Praise for The Blue Parakeet

We desperately need someone like Scot McKnight to bring balance and a healthy evangelical perspective about how we should view Scripture. To me, this book should be read by every Christian who takes Scripture seriously and is living missionally in the world. The questions he raises and addresses about the Bible are ones we urgently need to be thinking through and answering.

—DAN KIMBALL, pastor and author,
They Like Jesus but Not the Church

The Blue Parakeet is like no other book about the Bible I've ever read. I recommend it for everyone who reads, loves, struggles with, tries to teach or preach, follows, obeys, trusts, and sometimes questions the Bible. It challenges Christians to a more honest and mature engagement with Scripture, and it makes the wisdom of a seasoned theologian accessible to down-to-earth church-goers—seasoned generously with honesty, clarity, and a disarming humor too.

—BRIAN McLAREN, speaker and author,
A Generous Orthodoxy

For those who have spent a good deal of their Christian lives fruitlessly attempting to "cage" all those pesky "Blue Parakeet" passages in the Bible, Scot McKnight's "Third Way" of reading and applying the Scriptures comes as a welcome relief. With this refreshing and logical approach to God's Great Story, we can turn the pages of Scripture without dreading the tough passages and cultural divides, but rather appreciating them for their uniqueness, beauty, and truth as God intended from the beginning.

—ANDREW McQUITTY, senior pastor,
Irving Bible Church

In *The Blue Parakeet* Scot McKnight has expertly culled from the wisdom of the ages to show us that the B-I-B-L-E is more than just a literary work for scholars and theologians to argue over. It's an ongoing dialogue with the living God. Brother McKnight good-naturedly nudges us to listen up while God swaps his stories with us.

> —**Karen Spears-Zacharias**, author,
> *Where's Your Jesus Now?*

With a bold sensitivity and scholarly creativity, Scot McKnight challenges us to consider how we misuse the Bible, and he offers timely, targeted spiritual direction about encountering God together through God's story of grace.

> —**John W. Frye**, pastor and author,
> *Jesus the Pastor: Leading Others in the Character
> and Power of Christ*

The Blue Parakeet is the book Scot McKnight was born to write. If you are interested in the Bible, or God, or your mind, or where these three might intersect, you will be blessed if you read this book.

> —**John Ortberg**, pastor and author,
> *Faith and Doubt*

This is far and away the best, gentlest, most intelligent argument I have ever read for the absolute necessity of embracing the Bible as Story. McKnight is in full and persuasive command of both his material and his craft.

> —**Phyllis Tickle**, founding editor
> of the religion department of *Publishers Weekly*

the
Blue Parakeet

Rethinking How You
Read the Bible

Scot McKnight

ZONDERVAN

ZONDERVAN.com/
AUTHORTRACKER
follow your favorite authors

The Blue Parakeet
Copyright © 2008 by Scot McKnight

This title is also available as a Zondervan ebook.
Visit www.zondervan.com/ebooks.

Requests for information should be addressed to:

Zondervan, *Grand Rapids, Michigan 49530*

Library of Congress Cataloging-in-Publication Data

McKnight, Scot.
    The blue parakeet : rethinking how you read the Bible / Scot McKnight.
       p. cm.
    ISBN 978-0-310-28488-8 (hardcover, jacketed)
    1. Bible — Hermeneutics. 2. Bible — Criticism, Narrative. I. Title.
    BS476.M3473   2008
    220.601 — dc22   2008025226

Published in association with the literary agency of Daniel Literary Group, LLC, 1701 Kingsbury Drive, Suite 100, Nashville, TN 37215

Interior design by Beth Shagene

Printed in the United States of America

09 10 11 12 13 14 • 23 22 21 20 19 18 17 16 15 14 13 12 11 10 9 8 7 6 5 4 3 2

For Cheryl Hatch

Contents

He said to them, "Therefore every teacher of the law who has been instructed about the kingdom of heaven is like the owner of a house who brings out of his storeroom new treasures as well as old."

Jesus, according to Matthew 13:52

Blessed Lord, who caused all Holy Scriptures to be written for our learning: Grant me so to hear them, read, mark, learn, and inwardly digest them, that I may embrace and ever hold fast the blessed hope of everlasting life, which you have given us in our Savior Jesus Christ, who lives and reigns with you and the Holy Spirit, one God, for ever and ever. Amen. ✝

But when he, the Spirit of truth, comes, he will guide you into all the truth.

Jesus, according to John 16:13

Chapter 1

The Book and I

How, Then, Are We to Live
the Bible Today?

When I was in high school, I went to a Christian camp in Muscatine, Iowa, with Kris, my beautiful girlfriend (now my wife), to horse around for a week. But one morning, we were asked by our cabin leader to go spend a little time in prayer before breakfast. So I wandered out of our cabin, down a hill, alongside a basketball court, and through an open field, and then I walked over to the campfire area, climbed a short incline, and finally sat next to a tree, and prayed what my cabin leader told us to pray: "Lord, fill me with your Holy Spirit." I wasn't particularly open to spiritual things, but for some reason I said that prayer as our counselor advised. The Lord to whom I prayed that prayer caught me off guard. To quote the words of John Wesley, "My heart was strangely warmed." I don't remember what I expected to happen (probably nothing), but what happened was surprising. That prayer, or I should say the answer to that prayer, changed my life. I didn't speak in tongues, I didn't "see Jesus," and I didn't "hear God." My eyes didn't twitter, and I didn't become catatonic. When I prayed, something powerful happened, and I went to breakfast a new person. Within hours I knew what I wanted to do for my life.

On that hot summer day, I unexpectedly became a Bible student with a voracious appetite to read. Prior to that prayer I had very little interest in the Bible, and when it came to routine reading, I read only what my teachers assigned and *Sports Illustrated*. Within a week or two I began to read the Bible through from Genesis to Revelation, four chapters a day. I finished my reading the next spring, getting ahead of schedule because there were too many days when four chapters were not enough. My habit at the time was to arise early to read at least two chapters before going off to school, and then to read two chapters or so at night before I went to bed. I read the *Scofield King James Bible*, and Paul's letter to the Galatians became my favorite book. The Bible was full of surprises for me, and my eyes, mind, and heart were stuck on wide-open wonder. All because I asked God's Spirit to fill me.

Some of my former Sunday school teachers were as surprised as I was by what was happening. My youth pastor encouraged me to read serious books, and he also modeled a way to study the Bible by teaching Romans to our youth group. He also suggested I learn Greek, which, because he had a spare beginning Greek grammar book, I began. I had no idea what I was doing, but I liked languages, so I plugged away, never knowing quite what to expect. My father gave me some books to read, like John Bunyan's *Pilgrim's Progress*. I devoured books. My teachers observed that I read books for class, not because I had to, but to learn and to engage in conversation.

I had no idea what I was getting into when I asked God's Spirit to fill me. I had no idea that I would go to college in Grand Rapids and become a bookaholic, buying books with money I didn't have! I hung out at Eerdmans and Zondervan and Baker and Kregel looking for bargains. I knew the sales clerks by name and they knew mine. I had no idea that I would then go on to seminary and from there for doctoral studies in England (Nottingham). I had no idea how hard it might be to find a teaching position. But I have lived a privileged life, teaching at a seminary for a dozen years and now teaching undergraduates at North Park University for nearly fifteen years. I had no idea that I would eventually get to travel to and speak in churches around the world, that I would get to write books about Jesus and Paul and Peter and the Bible, and that I would become friends with Bible scholars all around the world. I just had no idea that teaching the Bible meant these things when I asked God's Spirit to fill me. All I know is that from the time I was converted, I wanted to study the Bible. I'm sitting right now in my study, surrounded by books, books about the Bible, and I love what I do. I just had no idea.

The Discovery of a Question

Throughout this process of conversion and reading the Bible, I made discoveries that created a question that disturbed me and still does. Many of my fine Christian friends, pastors, and teachers routinely made the claim that they were Bible-believing Christians, and they were committed to the whole Bible and that—and this was one of the favorite lines—"God said it, I believe it, that settles it for me!" They were saying two things and I add my response (which expresses my disturbance):

> One: We believe everything the Bible says, *therefore* . . .
> Two: We *practice* whatever the Bible says.
> Three: Hogwash!

Why say "hogwash," a tasty, salty word I learned from my father? Because I was reading the same Bible they were reading, and I observed that, in fact—emphasize that word "fact"—whatever they were claiming was not in "fact" what they were doing. (Nor was I.) What I discovered is that we all pick and choose. I must confess this discovery did not discourage me as much as it disturbed me, and then it made me intensely curious (and it is why I wrote this book). The discoveries and disturbances converged onto one big question:

> How, then, are we to live out the Bible today?

This question never has been and never will be adequately answered with: The Bible says it, and that settles it for me. Why? Because no one does everything the Bible says. Perhaps you expected this question: How, then, are we to *apply* the Bible today? That's a good question, but I think the word "apply" is a bit clinical and not as dynamic as the phrase "live out." But we will get to that later.

Here's an example of my discovery process as a young student of the Bible. When you and I read the letter of James, brother of Jesus, we hear these words:

> Those who consider themselves religious and yet do not keep a tight rein on their tongues deceive themselves, and their religion is worthless. Religion that God our Father accepts as pure and fault-less is this: to look after orphans and widows in their distress and to keep oneself from being polluted by the world. (James 1:26–27)

James knew what he was talking about, and, truth be told, there's nothing hard about understanding what James said. It's about as plain as the directions on a stop sign. The clarity of these words is the problem. For all kinds of reasons, and we'll get to those soon, what James said had almost nothing to do with the Christian groups I knew:

- We didn't like the word "religious."
- We didn't measure Christian maturity by control of the tongue (according to what I was hearing).
- Pure and faultless—and that's pretty high quality, you must admit—religion, according to James, isn't measured by church attendance, Bible reading, witnessing, going to seminary, or anything else I found in our discipleship and church membership manuals.

Nope, for James, a pure Christian, the kind God approves of, was one who showed compassion to orphans and widows and avoided being polluted by sin at all costs. Frankly, we emphasized the not being polluted by sin, but we defined "polluted" in ways that had nothing to do with compassion for the marginalized and suffering. For instance, we were dead set against movies, drinking wine, and sex before marriage. In our version of reality, these three were all related — if you drank with your girlfriend, you'd lose your senses and go to a movie and end up having sex. I'm not only making fun of my past, I'm emphasizing how distorted things got — a good, solid Christian was one who didn't do specific things that were against the rules. It also had to do with what we *did* — which was go to church weekly, read the Bible daily, and witness as often as we could. These aren't bad things; in fact, I learned to love the Bible because of this context. But the one thing we didn't do was follow everything James said!

As I kept looking around me, this began to disturb me. How in the world were we reading the same Bible? One thing was clear, we were all reading the Bible the same way, and that meant we had somehow learned not to follow the plain words of James.

What I learned was an uncomfortable but incredibly intriguing truth: Every one of us adopts the Bible and (at the same time) adapts the Bible to our culture. In less-appreciated terms, I'll put it this way: Everyone picks and chooses. I know this sounds out of the box and off the wall for many, but no matter how hard we try to convince ourselves otherwise, it's true. We pick and choose. (It's easier for us to hear "we adopt and adapt," but the two expressions amount to the same thing.)

I believe many of us want to know *why* we pick and choose. Even more importantly, many of us want to know *how to do this in a way that honors God and embraces the Bible as God's Word for all times.* We'll get to that. First, I offer some examples of picking and choosing, or "adopting and adapting."

Picking and Choosing

Sabbath

The Bible I read both instituted and did not appear to back down from the *Sabbath*. Observing the Sabbath meant not working from Friday night to Saturday night (Exodus 20:9 – 10), and I found numerous references in the Acts of the Apostles to the Christian observance of Sabbath. But as I was learning how to read the Bible inside a bundle of serious-minded Christians, I knew no one who really practiced the Sabbath. I quickly learned that the Christian Sunday, which focuses on fellowship and worship, is not the same as the Jewish Sabbath, which focuses on rest from labor. (You can read about this in any good Bible dictionary or on Wikipedia.) The Sabbath was described in the Bible, and it wasn't a "that settles it for me!" for anyone I knew.

What really got me going was that nobody seemed interested in this question. Yes, I did hear that some thought a passage like Colossians 2:16 may — but only *may* — have given Gentiles permission not to keep Sabbath, but the issue was not crystal clear. I was learning that we sometimes, rightly or wrongly, live out the Bible by *not doing* something in the Bible![1]

Tithing

The Bible I read taught *tithing*, but the Bible does not insist that all of the tithe must go to a local church. Truth be told, the New Testament doesn't even bring up the tithe. In the Bible the tithe is a combination of spiritual support (for the temple) and social service (for the poor). Moses says tithes are to be given not only to the Levites (roughly the temple servants) but also to the alien, to the fatherless, and to the widow (Deuteronomy 26:12). The churches I was attending had nothing to do with immigrants, did little to help orphans, and so far as I knew did little to strengthen widows.

What was more, the tithe we were hearing about was something we were to give to our local church for buildings, maintenance, pastoral salaries, missionaries, and the like. But the Bible said that I — as a tither — was to give some of my tithe to the Levite and also to those who were marginalized and suffering. This was something neither I nor anyone I knew was doing. I was learning that we sometimes live out the Bible, rightly or wrongly, by *morphing* one thing into another, that is, by taking a tithe for temple assistants and also for the poor and turning it into a tithe for the local church. It might be fine to read the Bible like this, but we should at least admit what we are doing: in a word, we are morphing.

Foot Washing

Another discovery I made was that Jesus explicitly commanded *foot washing* in John 13:14. Widows who received benefits from the church were known as those who had washed the feet of saints (1 Timothy 5:10). St. Augustine, three and a half centuries later, writes about Christians washing the feet of the freshly baptized, so I knew that the practice continued well beyond the New Testament days. But I was surrounded by Bible believers and had never seen this happen. I learned that some Christians still practice this, but no one I knew (except a high school friend's church) was doing it. We were either ignoring what the Bible taught or morphing it into a cultural parallel like hanging up one another's coats and offering our guests something to drink. A New Testament scholar, Bill Mounce, in his exhaustive study of 1 Timothy, draws this conclusion about what Paul says of widows: "Paul is not asking if the widow followed church ritual [physically washed feet]; he is asking if she was the type of person who had done good deeds throughout her life."[2] In other words, Paul is not speaking of something literal—real washing of feet—but of an underlying principle— serving others. What I learned is that sometimes we *look behind the text to grasp a timeless principle and the principle is more important than doing the actual words.*

Bill Mounce might be right, but my question as a college student was this one: "How did we know Paul's words were really only describing a symptom of a person of good deeds instead of a literal requirement?" Some suggested to me to quit asking such pesky questions and just follow along, but inside I was learning to ask what for me has a been a lifelong joyous ride of exploring how we live out the Bible.

Charismatic Gifts

The more I became aware of the rise of the charismatic movement, the more I discovered Jesus, Paul, and Peter had the power to work *miracles* (Matthew 4:23; 10:8; Acts 4:1–12; 16:16–18). In my first year of Bible reading I learned that Christians in Paul's churches *gave words of prophecy* (1 Corinthians 12–14). And I knew Jesus said that his followers would do even greater things than he did. No one that I knew was doing miracles or giving words of prophecy. What I learned from this experience is an expression that sums up the way many read the Bible: *"that was then, but this is now."*

In other words, I learned that God spoke in various ways in various times. And I was taught that God wasn't saying *those* things today. I was only beginning to wonder just how enormous a dragon that little expression — "that was then, but this is now" — was hiding. I learned that sometimes *the Bible expects things that were designed for that time but not for our time.* I wasn't sure how we knew that, but I was sure we were making decisions like that. This really sealed my question: How do we know how to live out the Bible? But there are a few more examples for us to consider.

Surrendering Possessions

There is nothing clearer than this statement by Jesus about *possessions*: "In the same way, those of you who do not give up everything you have [possessions] cannot be my disciples" (Luke 14:33). Two chapters earlier Jesus said, "Sell your possessions and give to the poor" (12:33). If there is anything that is straightforward, those two verses are. I knew enough about church history to know that St. Francis did exactly what Jesus ordered, or at least he got very close. I also knew that we weren't following Jesus' words at all. In fact, I knew that most Christians were not living below their means and were in fact living well beyond their means.

The most common explanations I heard were either "but that was then" or "there were special expectations for Jesus' personal disciples." Others suggested that what we could take away from these statements by Jesus was that we should "cut back" on our spending so we can be more generous. However we read them, these are statements made by Jesus, seemingly without condition; we weren't doing them as Jesus said; and they evidently belonged to a different era and a different culture (this principle kept coming up). How did we decide such things? How do we know what to do and what not to do? (I can't tell you how much these two questions have energized my thirty-plus years of Bible study.)

Contentious Issues

On top of these discoveries I was encountering *contentious issues* like evolution, Calvinism, Vietnam and war, abortion, and homosexuality. I must confess I loved the thrill of these debates. These hotly disputed issues took some of these discoveries of mine and stood them up into questions — questions of practical and present significance, questions that started to mound up into my one big question:

> Do we conform the Bible to science, science to the Bible, or ...?
> Is Calvinism or Arminianism right? Are both right? Is neither right?
> What kind of music should we play in church? (God bless Larry Norman and Cliff Richard.)
> Are the charismatic gifts relevant today? All of them? Even miracles?
> Should we oppose the conflict in Vietnam?
> Which view of the second coming is biblical?
> Should women be ordained? Can they preach and teach?
> What do we do about abortion?
> What do we do about capital punishment and nuclear war?
> Is homosexual behavior a sin?

And they became the one big question for me: How, then, are we to live out the Bible today?

The Question Is "How?"

What made me so curious and what gave me a deep discontent was *how* we came to our answers. Some people went straight to the Bible and stayed there; some people took one passage and overwhelmed another; yet others read the Bible, appealing to history and change and then to theologians, science, pastors, psychologists, and even to "that's the way we do things at my church." I began to see that Christians read the Bible differently and I began to see that no one group seemed to get it all right. At that time in my life I was asking questions like these:

> Why is it that one group thinks the charismatic gifts are dead and gone while other groups vibrate with tongue-speaking and words of prophecy?
> Why is it that two of us can sit down with the same Bible with the same question—Should Christians participate in war?—and come away with two different answers? One can appeal to Joshua and Judges and the other can appeal to Jesus' statement to love your enemies and to turn the other cheek.
> Why do some churches ordain women and let them preach while other churches have folks who get up and walk out when a woman opens her Bible for some teaching in front of men?

As a faithful attendee of churches, as one fully committed to the faith, as one who read his Bible daily, and as one who watched and listened to debates unroll and even unravel, I became convinced that it was not so easy to "apply" the Bible as I thought it was. In fact, when it came to contentious issues, how we read the Bible discerns how we are to live. To be perfectly honest to this young student of the Bible, I knew there was plenty of picking and choosing *on both sides of every question.* I pressed on for two more decades and I have now come to the conclusion that this question—How, then, are we to live out the Bible today?—is a pressing question for our day. I believe we need to begin asking this question and "start splainin' ourselves." I believe there is an inner logic to our picking and choosing, but I believe we need to become aware of what it is.

Until we do, we will be open to accusations of hypocrisy. It's that simple, and it's that lethal. If you tell me you believe the Bible and seek to live out every bit of it, and if I can find one spot that you don't — especially if that spot is sensitive or politically incorrect or offensive — then we've all got a problem. I teach college students the Bible, and I can assure you that they are fully aware of the "pick-and-choose" method. They are fully convinced, at least many of them, that the pick-and-choose method is an exercise in hypocrisy or worse.

What I've learned is this: *People are afraid of this question once they turn it inside out on themselves and others.* Too many of us don't want to think about this. Too many of us don't want to admit that we are picking and choosing. Even if we prefer (as I do) to say "adopting and adapting," we are doing something similar. But I think we need to face this squarely and honestly. I've learned that it is time to think about why and how we pick what we pick and why and how we choose what we choose. What can we do to get ourselves to face this question honestly?

What Will It Take to Get Us to Ask This Question?

Sometimes it is a classroom setting that provokes this question. I once had a student ask me point-blank in class a question about this passage: "As you go, proclaim this message: 'The kingdom of heaven has come near.' Heal the sick, raise the dead, cleanse those who have leprosy, drive out demons."

"Yo, Scot." [Evidently "Yo" now means "Dr."] "Yo, Scot, since you believe we should preach the kingdom of God today, as Jesus said in Matthew 10:7, why don't you also believe we should heal the sick as in Matthew 10:8?" What he was asking me, in his playful snarky way, was why I pick one to do and choose not to do the other. I have done lots of verse 7 but have never done any of verse 8. He had me, but it was one of those moments when I got to ask my favorite question: How, then, are we to live out the Bible today?

There's a story here, as there so often is. Joel Martens, the student, is an active member in a Vineyard Church where charismatic gifts are emphasized. I wasn't either Vineyard or charismatic (though I always say "I'm open!"). Does that mean he's given to exaggerating or that I'm given to minimizing Matthew 10:8? You answer the question. When I talked to Kris about this classroom experience, she asked why I didn't ask him, "Do you raise the dead at your church?" You can answer that one, too. (When I see Joel next, I'll ask him in a snarky way.) Anyway, Joel got our class thinking about this question and his question hasn't yet gone away for me.

More often than not it is a *person* who enters into our world that shakes up our thinking that gets us asking this question. Perhaps we encounter someone who speaks in tongues or someone who thinks they can heal others or a friend's daughter who is a lesbian and also a Christian. It's one thing to say we think homosexuality is sin, but it's completely different when we know a gay or a lesbian and that someone happens to ask us why we believe in Leviticus 20:13a but not in 20:13b—the first prohibits homosexuality and the second insists on capital punishment for it. Or if we are asked why we think the instruction from *nature* in Romans 1 about homosexuality is permanent and applicable today, but the one in 1 Corinthians 11 is evidently disposable.

Here's what Paul says about "nature" in Romans 1:26: "Even their women exchanged *natural* sexual relations for *unnatural* ones." But those same persons don't think Paul's instructions about *nature* in 1 Corinthians 11:14 are permanent: "Does not the very *nature* of things teach you that if a man has long hair, it is a disgrace to him, but that if a woman has long hair, it is her glory?" (emphasis added in both passages). So, a lesbian asks why some embrace the appeal to "nature" in Romans 1 while our wives have short hair and our sons have hair pulled back into a ponytail. Again, before you answer that question, it would be really good if you pulled up to a coffee table with a few friends and opened up your Bible to these passages and asked yourselves this question: How, then, are we to live out the Bible today?

By such personal encounters we are driven to think aloud about what we believe, we are driven to think more carefully about what we think, we are driven back to the Bible and how we read it, we are driven to ask how it is that we are living out the Bible, and we are sometimes driven to our knees to ask for wisdom about contentious issues. One such issue, which will be the focus of the last part of this book, is the giftedness of women for various ministries in the church, including teaching and preaching and pastoring.

Perhaps we need a visitor to come by, and maybe this book will be that visitor, who gets us to ask this question. I believe we need to ask the question and, together, begin to work it out.

Chapter 2

The Birds and I

Which Way Do You Read the Bible?

Kris and I are both birdwatchers, something we absorbed from Kris's Grandma Norman and Kris's father, Ron Norman, so we have a few birdfeeders in our backyard. Which means, whether we like it or not, we feed sparrows and chase or throw things at squirrels. You know you are a birder if you chase squirrels from your feeders by running through the yard, yelling wildly, and squirting them with the water pistol you bought for your grandson's birthday next month. You know you are even more of a birder if you decide to keep the water pistol you bought for your grandson's birthday and get him another gift because squirting squirrels is both effective and a whole lot of fun.[1]

Squirrels are a problem, but so are sparrows. If we could get rid of sparrows we would, because we prefer the cardinals, goldfinches, and chickadees, and we'd love it if some cedar waxwings would visit us. But sparrows are omnipresent in our yard, sometimes as many as fifty of them fighting for places on our feeders and knocking perfectly good seed onto the ground while they look for the perfect little chunk. Because we've been watching birds for about thirty years, we've become adept at recognizing them. It is unusual when we see a bird we don't instantly recognize. At times we'll see a rare visitor, like a white-throated sparrow or a rose-breasted grosbeak or a migrating warbler, but not very often.

Sitting on my back porch reading in the summer of 2007 and looking up, I happened to observe a flash of soft blue in the bushes next to our fencerow. I didn't see the whole bird. Only part of it was visible through the green leaves. I got to wondering and thinking and my bird-watching skills kicked in and I said — and any birder will tell you this is how it happens, so don't think there's anything special here: "Not a blue jay, too small; not an eastern bluebird, the blue is too soft; not an indigo bunting, it is too large and the colors too soft." I thought to myself, now beginning to look for those distinguishing marks that separate one bird from another, "What kind of a blue bird is this? Could it be a stray mountain bluebird?" But no, I thought, that's not possible. Mountain bluebirds don't wander from the Rockies into the Great Lakes regions during the summer.

Then the bluish bird moved itself a bit, I stretched my neck to look closer and I caught full view of it. I was disappointed. It was someone's pet blue parakeet. It had escaped its cage and was now a free bird. Tempted to ignore it — after all, it was nothing but a stray pet — I began to take note of its manners. Odd thing, this chance encounter. I started to wonder how it would behave and it got me to comparing its behavior with the other birds in our yard.

The first thing I observed was immediate: our sparrows were — and no other word describes their response — terrorized by our visitor the blue parakeet. When it moved even a little, the sparrows scattered like teenage pranksters when a cop car wanders into the neighborhood. When it flew, the sparrows were scared witless again and scattered into hiding in other bushes or to find distance from it on telephone lines. When it decided to let out its obnoxious sound, they were once again frightened to fly away. Odd, I thought to myself, for the sparrows to be so fearful of a pet bird. Even if they scattered easily, they eventually found their way back to their usual locations. Instead of reading my book, I had become a full-time wonderer about bird behaviors.

The inhospitality of our sparrows to our visitor bothered me, so I got up from my comfortable seat, went inside, found my Franciscan brown habit, tied up the rope around my waist, and went back on the back porch and preached—à la St. Francis according to Giotto—to our sparrows about how to treat visitors. (I really didn't do this but I grew up Baptist, and we permit making things up as long as it is "preacher's license.") Anyway, the sparrows were scared and I was learning.

I was now hooked on backyard social ethics when an odd sort of social miracle occurred before my eyes. The sparrows gradually became accustomed to the blue parakeet. Instead of being shocked by the odd sounds and sudden flights of the parakeet, they gradually became unfazed. In fact, they not only got used to the parakeet, they became best friends, what my daughter Laura calls "BFFs." When it flew to the feeder, they joined it—not because they were hungry, but because they wanted to be near the blue parakeet. When it flew to the neighbor's roof, they followed. One time I saw about thirty sparrows surrounding the blue parakeet on the neighbor's garage.

Within an hour, the sparrows had either trained the blue parakeet into their ways, or, what is more likely, they adjusted themselves so that the parakeet's ways were familiar. They didn't try to teach it to fly as they did (which is a good thing), nor did they silence its funny sounds (which is also a good thing). They let the blue parakeet be a blue parakeet. So, our visitor maintained that obnoxious squawk and flew with glorious speed and capacity to take sharp turns and sudden dips unlike the sparrows had ever seen. The sparrows may have thought they had adjusted, but every now and then that blue parakeet—and he stayed around for about a month—did something that frightened even the familiarized sparrows. The blue parakeet, like Narnia's Aslan, was not tame, but it became a familiar stranger to our sparrows.

Chance encounters sometimes lead us deeper into thought. The passages I mentioned in the previous chapter as well as comments from students are for me "blue parakeet experiences." When we encounter blue parakeets in the Bible or in the questions of others, whether we think of something as simple as the Sabbath or foot washing or as complex and emotional as women in church ministries or homosexuality, we have to stop and think. Is this passage for today or not? Sometimes we hope the blue parakeets will go away—as I hoped. After all, it was just a pet. Or perhaps we shoo them away. Or perhaps we try to catch them and return them to their cage. I tried to see if I could catch the bird, but he (or she) didn't even let me get close. It had been caged and it wanted its freedom.

How we respond to passages and questions will determine if we become aware of what is going on or not. When chance encounters with blue parakeet passages in the Bible happen to come our way, we are given the opportunity to observe and learn. In such cases, we really do open ourselves to the thrill of learning how to read the Bible. But, like the sparrows, we have to get over our fears and learn to adjust to the squawks of the Bible's blue parakeets. We dare not tame them.

How do you read the Bible? What happens to you when you encounter blue parakeet passages in the Bible will reveal all you need to know about how you read the Bible. I want to suggest there are three ways to approach the Bible.

Three Ways

There are actually more than three ways, but getting every possible option on the table is not important right now. If you'd like to think more about this, Appendix 1 is a quiz that many say creates all kinds of thinking about how to read the Bible. I have chosen to keep the ways simple in order to see the alternatives more starkly. Most people combine these ways, but most people are also often not aware of the way they read the Bible.

1. Reading to Retrieve

Some of us have been taught to read the Bible in such a way that we *return to the times of the Bible in order to retrieve biblical ideas and practices for today.* There are two kinds of "return and retrieve" readers—some try to retrieve *all of it* and some admit we can retrieve only *what can be salvaged.*

Consider those who seek to retrieve *all of it.* If Jesus taught table fellowship, such persons sometimes suggest that we should focus on table fellowship and gather in homes instead of big churches. If Paul said we should speak in tongues, we should speak in tongues. If Jesus said we should wash feet, we should wash feet. If Peter says women should not wear gold jewelry or fine clothing, our women should not wear gold jewelry or fine clothing. If Paul says women should be silent, our women should be silent. If Exodus says the death penalty is proper, then it is proper today too (even for adulterers). If Deuteronomy exhorts the Israelites to permit the poor to glean from the crops, then we should at least find a cultural equivalent. In other words, we are to live out the Bible today by *returning to the early church and retrieving all its ideas no matter how uncomfortable, no matter how politically incorrect, no matter what it costs us.* The emphasis here is to practice *whatever* the Bible teaches—to absorb and live out *all of it.*

There are some problems here. If we sit down and think about it, it is *impossible* to live a first-century life in a twenty-first-century world. "That was then, but this is now" is not an empty slogan that came my way to dismiss my questions as a college student. "That was then, but this is now" is bedrock reality. Furthermore, it is *undesirable and unbiblical* to retrieve it all. Paul didn't even do that. What about the words of the apostle Paul in 1 Corinthians 9:19–23, where Paul says his strategy is one of constant adaptation? Paul's strategy was to be Jewish with Jews and to be like a Gentile with Gentiles. If Paul was already adapting first-century Jewish ideas to first-century Gentile situations, can we expect to do anything else? Can we imagine Paul wanting to back up in time to Moses' day? To quote Paul, "By no means!"

What we've got in the pages of the New Testament are first-century expressions of the gospel and church life, not permanent, timeless expressions. They are timely expressions; they are Spirit-inspired expressions; but they were and remain first-century expressions. We aren't called to live first-century lives in the twenty-first century, *but twenty-first-century lives as we walk in the light of the revelation God gave to us in the first century.*

For some, and you may be one of them, this principle sounds like we are giving away too much. Some believe we are to return to the Bible, but we can retrieve only *what we can salvage for our day and for our culture.* This, of course, means culture dictates what is of value in the Bible. This is a mistake. But, before we say anything else, I want to applaud anyone and everyone who tries to bring the Bible into our modern culture. This is the impulse of the apostle Paul—and we see it in all of the New Testament writers who adopted the Story and adapted it to their contexts. I can think of a list of creative Christian thinkers today who are exceptional at adopting and adapting, but I'll avoid listing names.

The danger in "retrieving the essence" is there can be too little adoption or not enough faithfulness and consistency with the Bible itself. Take women in church ministries as an example. Some contend that the argument over women pastors is a *justice* issue, and by that they mean equality, rights, freedom, and centuries of oppression. While I have respect for the "justice" issue when it comes to women in church ministries today (the last section of this book will make this clear), I'm not so sure we are to judge what goes on in the church by the principles of our culture: "equality" and "rights" and "freedom." In fact, I'm certain this is not the way we are called by God to "apply" the Bible to our world—there is more to it than letting culture shape what we do. Before we go any further, we need to insert a parenthetical observation about Bible reading.

Those Days, Those Ways

One of the themes we will encounter in this book can be summed up like this:

> God spoke in Moses' days in Moses' ways, and
> God spoke in Job's days in Job's ways, and

> God spoke in David's days in David's ways, and
> God spoke in Solomon's days in Solomon's ways, and
> God spoke in Jeremiah's days in Jeremiah's ways, and
> God spoke in Jesus' days in Jesus' ways, and
> God spoke in Paul's days in Paul's ways, and
> God spoke in Peter's days in Peter's ways, and
> God spoke in John's days in John's ways,
> *and we are called to carry on that pattern in our world today.*

The gospel is capable and designed to strike home in every culture, in every age, and in every language. Any idea of imposing a foreign culture, age, or language on another culture, age, and language quenches the dynamic power of the gospel and the Bible. We need not become Jews to live the gospel, nor need we become first- or fourth- or sixteenth- or eighteenth-century Christians. Let me push hard for a moment. Yes, I think the first Jewish Christians probably kept kosher. That's not for today. Yes, the vestments of the Eastern Orthodox Church are brilliant and the liturgical order of services profound — but they are from a bygone era, with a bygone dress code, and a bygone form of expression, and do precious little for most of us today. They are not for today (at least for most of us). Yes, I love the history they unveil. If I appreciate and respect that history, that does not mean I have to live in those days now. I also love European cathedrals — monuments to the piety of a former era. Those cathedrals, apart from tourists and the rare exception, are empty today. I also love Martin Luther, John Calvin, and Jonathan Edwards, and they were leaders for their days in their ways. But I have no desire to impose their culture on our days and our ways. Frankly, I'm more concerned with their attitudes.

What we most need is not a return to the first or fourth or sixteenth or eighteenth century but a fresh blowing of God's Spirit on our culture, in our day, and in our ways. We need twenty-first-century Christians living out the biblical gospel in twenty-first-century ways. Even more, if we read the Bible properly, we will see that God never asked one generation to step back in time and live the way it had done before. No, God spoke in each generation in that generation's ways.

Most of us know one of the major failures of missionary work was the unfortunate (if naïve and good-intentioned) imposing of Western ways on African or Asian ways. We now know that the gospel has the power to generate expressions of the gospel in every language, in every culture, and in every ethnic group. If we know this about current missionary work, doesn't that warn us about the danger of returning in order to retrieve it all? Next to my desk is a commentary on the entire Bible called *Africa Bible Commentary.*[2] The aim here was to write a commentary on the Bible by Africans for Africans instead of a commentary for Africans by Americans. The apostle Paul would have been the first one to stand in applause of this effort. I can't resist. Next to that Bible commentary I have a book called *The IVP Women's Bible Commentary* — by women for women.[3] And, yes, I think Paul would applaud that too.

The way of returning to retrieve it all is not the biblical way. The biblical way is the ongoing adoption of the past and adaptation to new conditions and to do this in a way that is *consistent with and faithful to the Bible.* I've been teaching this idea for a long time, and I have learned to anticipate the next question: Who decides on what to adopt and how to adapt? Will it be you alone, will it be you and your friends, will it be you and your pastor, will it be your pastor and the elders, or will it be your denominational leaders? Will it be the Pope or the Patriarch? Who decides? This just might be the million dollar question that will determine how you will live out the Bible today, and it leads to a second way we are reading the Bible so we can live it out today.

2. Reading through Tradition

We need to do a little work before we get to the main point of this section, but our overall point is this: ordinary people need to learn to read the Bible *through* tradition or they will misread the Bible and create schisms in the church.

The most alarming danger of the "return and retrieve" way of Bible reading is found throughout the Western world: it seems too often that *everybody reads the Bible for herself or for himself, and everybody does what's right in her or his own eyes.* We see this in three groups. *Pastors* have come up with their own pet theory for how to read the Bible that no one in the history of the church has ever seen. *Books and catalogs* cross my desk daily with new ideas, and often they are advertised as an idea that's fresh, insightful, never-been-seen-before-but-straight-from-the-Bible, yada yada yada. Engaging with Christian Bible readers over the years leads me to the third group: God bless 'em, but *some folks* see some of the goofiest things in the Bible, and I wish I could just blow Holy-Spirit-air on them and cure them of their silliness.

Before I say another word, though, I must confess: I believe we are called to read the Bible for ourselves. (But not entirely on our own.) The Reformation's best and *most dangerous, revolutionary idea* was putting the Bible in the hands of ordinary Christians. One of John Calvin's deepest desires in the Reformation was to provide the tools for ordinary Christians to read the Bible by themselves. So what did he do? For pastors, he wrote his famous *Institutes of the Christian Religion* and his extensive *commentaries on the Bible*, and for laypeople he designed a *catechism* and wrote more lay-level *expositions*. He did this so that ordinary Christians could both read and understand the Bible. In this way, he believed, rightly, that the fires of revival could be set loose. But what strikes me about Calvin's plan was that he didn't just plop Bibles into the laps of everyone and say, "Here, read this! Nothing to it! Tell me what you think!" No, he wanted them to learn the Bible right, and to do that they would have to learn some basic theology.

I believe everyone should read the Bible, but no one has ever said that everyone should interpret the Bible for themselves and whatever they come up with is as good as anyone else's views. I now appeal to the other great reformer, Martin Luther. No one wanted the Bible in the hands of ordinary Germans more than Martin Luther. But Luther knew that bad interpretations create schisms and problems. What did he do? He wouldn't let schoolchildren read the Bible until they had mastered his *Catechism*. Even if you think he was being too strong here (and I do), it should reveal that no matter how much the Reformers wanted to place a Bible on the dinner table of every Christian, they also wanted to provide the readers with a sound method and theology that would lead them to read the Bible accurately. Sadly, in our world today many have neglected this Reformation strategy.

Because of this neglect, we are now living in a church with a myriad of interpreters. And it has caused a mighty reaction today with many evangelical Christians bolting for more traditional churches. The major current in this stream is the appeal to *tradition*. There are two senses of tradition here, one that I adhere to strongly (Great Tradition) and one that repels me (traditionalism). The first is the Great Tradition. The Great Tradition is how the church everywhere has always read the Bible. There is a wonderful evangelical resurgence today of returning to the Great Tradition of the church, and I mention three examples: Thomas Oden's *The Rebirth of Orthodoxy*, J. I. Packer's and Thomas Oden's *One Faith*, and Charles Colson's *The Faith*.[4] Each of these is calling Christians to the core doctrines that the faithful in the church have always believed. They are urging evangelicals especially to take more seriously what I am calling the Great Tradition.

That is, we may learn to read the Bible for ourselves, but we must be responsible to what the church has always believed. We can reduce the Great Tradition to the Nicene Creed, the Apostles' Creed, and the importance of justification by faith from the Reformation. These creeds point us toward the nonnegotiables of the faith; they point us to what God has led the church to see as its most important doctrines.

Some are going farther than this, though, and are giving too much authority to tradition. They are saying we need to read the Bible *through* tradition. The singular problem here is *traditionalism*. Traditionalism is the inflexible, don't-ask-questions, do-it-the-way-it-has-always-been-done approach to Bible reading. It reads the Bible *through* tradition. What happens then? Those who read the Bible *through* tradition always see the traditional way of reading the Bible. This approach is nearly incapable of renewal and adaptation.

What do we mean then by traditionalism? There are about six steps in this approach, and it occurs in every church and denomination I've been around. Rest assured, traditionalism occurs everywhere. You might say it's human nature. Here are the six steps, leading to traditionalism:

Step 1: We read the Bible.

Step 2: We confront a current issue and we make a decision about an issue — like baptizing infants or adults — or we frame "what we believe" into a confession, a creed, or a doctrinal statement.

Step 3: We *fossilize* our decision and it becomes a tradition.

(Somewhere around here we become absolutely convinced our tradition is a perfect interpretation of the Bible.)

Step 4: We are bound to our tradition forever.

(It is now *traditionalism*.)

Step 5: We are bound to read the Bible *through* our tradition.

(Somewhere around here we become convinced that God's Spirit led us to our tradition and that it is nothing less than an accurate, God-prompted, don't-question-it unfolding in history of what God's Word says.)

Step 6: Those who question our tradition are suspect or, worse yet, kicked out of our church.

(Somewhere around here we become ineffective in our world and become increasingly cantankerous about how the youth are wandering away from the faith.)

The Bible itself points us away from traditionalism. The biblical authors and the early fathers didn't fossilize traditions. Instead — and here we come to a major moment in this book — *they went back to the Bible so they could come forward into the present.* They did not go back to stay there (the "retrieve-it-all" tendency); they didn't dismiss the Bible easily (the "retrieve-only-the-essence" approach); and they didn't fossilize their discernments (traditionalism). Instead, each one went back to the Bible, to God's Word, so they could come forward into their own day in their own ways. This explains the variety of expressions from Genesis to Revelation; it alone explains how Paul and Peter could preach and preach and hardly quote a word of Jesus. It wasn't because they didn't know the words of Jesus. No, it was because they knew them so well they could renew Jesus' message in their day in their own ways — as God's Spirit prompted them.

I believe it is important to live within the Great Tradition and to interpret the Bible alongside that Great Tradition, but I also believe it has become nearly impossible for fossilization and traditionalism not to creep in. Is there a third way, a way that both returns to retrieve and also respects the Great Tradition? I believe there is, and it is the way of ongoing and constant *renewal* that returns, retrieves, and renews by reading the Bible *with* the Great Tradition.

3. Reading with Tradition

God was on the move; God is on the move; and God will always be on the move. Those who walk with God and listen to God are also on the move. Reading the Bible so we can live it out today means being on the move — always. Anyone who stops and wants to turn a particular moment into a monument, as the disciples did when Jesus was transfigured before them, will soon be wondering where God has gone.

In the sixteenth century the citizens of the Italian city of Lucca, in Tuscany, sensed their security was threatened by the mighty nobles of both Pisa (famous for its leaning tower) and Florence (famous for what my dear wife, Kris, calls its "pictures"). The Lucchesi (folks from Lucca) hatched a plan in response to these surrounding threats — transform their thin walls into impregnable walls. So, for one entire century 30 percent or more of the taxes were used to fund the new walls. The Lucchesi built a tall and squat, one-hundred-foot-wide wall of dirt, buttressed on each side with bricks. The irony of the story is that neither the Florentines nor the Pisans ever attacked Lucca. Happily, that wall did serve the Lucchesi by holding back a flood in 1812. Today, visitors to Lucca enjoy the 2.5-mile walk around the city atop the wall.

This wall might illustrate what happens when we convert the genius of a generation into fossilized, inflexible tradition. The wall, though it does get tourists like Kris and me to walk its entire length, is in the way. It is like reading the Bible *through* tradition. First you must scale it, traverse it, and descend it before you even have a chance of enjoying the inside of the city.

So, how can we read the Bible that is both a "return and retrieval" reading as well as being respectful of the Great Tradition? I suggest we learn to read the Bible *with* the Great Tradition. We dare not ignore what God has said to the church through the ages (as the return and retrieval folks often do), nor dare we fossilize past interpretations into traditionalism. Instead, *we need to go back to the Bible so we can move forward through the church and speak God's Word in our days in our ways.* We need to go back without getting stuck (the return problem), and we need to move forward without fossilizing our ideas (traditionalism). We want to walk between these two approaches. It's not easy, but I contend that the best of the evangelical approaches to the Bible and the best way of living the Bible today is to walk between these approaches. It is a third way.

In this approach we are to give the Bible primacy, like the "return and retrieval" crowd and the Reformers and (too often) unlike the traditionalists. The traditionalist approach too often swallows up the Bible with its tradition. But we are also to move forward by *setting the Bible loose to renew and keep on renewing* who we are, what we think, how we express the gospel, and how we live out the gospel in our world. But, unlike traditionalists, we don't freeze or fossilize our expressions of the gospel. What we decide is our way for our day. We expect the next generation to do the same. Reading the Bible *with* the Tradition gives us guidance but it also gives us freedom to differ with Tradition. In the last part of this book I will provide an example to show that reading the Bible *with* Tradition sometimes means we will disagree with the Tradition even if we respect it.

Is there a danger here, too? This approach, because it loves to return to the Bible, can easily slide into hyper-innovation. And, because it reads the Bible *with* Tradition, it can also fall prey to traditionalism. So, what can we do to avoid this hyperinnovation weakness? It's simple, and we are seeing more and more today who are doing it. We need to have *profound respect* for our past without giving it the final authority. I believe the final decision should always rest with the Scripture. Not so much respect that we fall into traditionalism, but enough to slow us down to ask how God has spoken to the church in the past. We show serious respect for our past when we learn our church history, when we learn how major leaders read the Bible in the past, and when we bring their voices to the table as we learn how to read the Bible for our time.[5]

Recently Kris and I attended a local Episcopalian church, St. Lawrence. I have long loved the Anglican *Book of Common Prayer* with its ordered service, meaningful readings of Scripture, and profound prayers. Most importantly, every Anglican service climaxes in the Lord's Supper, the Eucharist. Kris and I both enjoyed the worship deeply. As we drove away, I shared with Kris a thought that had dawned on me as I found myself immersed in the worship at St. Lawrence: "I am," I told her, "a Willopalian." I believe in the importance of a commitment both to the Great Tradition and to ongoing creative renewal we find in places like Willow Creek in South Barrington, Illinois.

Renewal carries forward God's timeless and historic message in a timely and cultured way for our day. We know that what we discern for our day is timely but not timeless. Making timeliness timeless is fossilizing. Our task is to take the timely timelessness of the Bible and make it timely timeliness for our world. We need to go back to the Bible's timely timelessness so we can come forward to live out the Bible in our timely timeliness. (Don't try to say that too fast.) You might say this is a "Willopalian" approach to reading the Bible.

The Bible and I Story Continued

I have to make a confession. Somewhere along the line when I learned to read the Bible and when I was coming to terms with my own question, during seminary and doctoral research, my wide-eyed wonder of Scripture diminished and the jaw-dropping surprises were fewer and farther between. My desire to master the Bible and put it all together into my own system drained the Bible of its raw, edgy, and strange elixirs. I was caging and taming my blue parakeets.

Many Bible teachers go through a period when teaching the Bible is a job and studying theology seems to do little more than put bread on the table. Many of us will admit that at times the mystery, the thrill, and the intoxicating attractions fade. But most of us, and this happened for me, come out the other end of that dimly lit and foggy tunnel to find the light. Some call this life beyond the tunnel a "second naïveté." While teaching undergraduates, and this was more of a process than an event, I gave up mastering the blue parakeets and began once again to listen to the Bible. The combination of students asking questions and those startling blue parakeet passages in the Bible awakened in me my earlier passions. Once again, as if drinking some eternal ambrosia, I found renewal and a renewing joy in the good news. I began to hear the blue parakeets again. The question came back with full force, and I embraced it as my own.

I now have no desire to tame blue parakeets. The Bible is what the Bible is, and I believe it. "Let the Bible be the Bible" is my motto, because teaching the Bible has taught me that the Bible will do its own work if we get out of the way and let it. Someone once said that the Bible needs no more defending than a lion, and I agree.

I have learned that when we take our hands off the pages of the Bible, read and listen to its words, and enter into its story by faith, something happens. It renews and continues to renew its powers. It becomes what it was meant to be, something both more intimate than an old pair of jeans and more unusual than alien creatures, something like a familiar stranger or an unpredictable neighbor or a pet lion whose presence invigorates its surroundings. Something like the glory of the ocean, which on the surface appears gentle and strolling and pleasant to observe, but under that surface there's a vibrant, teeming, swirling, dynamic world full of beauty and wonder. Or perhaps listening to the Bible is like having the most powerful person in the world sit down with you for coffee as a friend and chat with you.

Join me as we enter into the world of reading the Bible in such a way that it comes to life for us, in such a way that it is renewing and ever renewing, in such a way that we learn how to live it out. Three words tell us how to read the Bible and we will devote a section to each:

Story

Listening

Discerning

That's all we need to know. It's all in those three words.

Part I

Story

What Is the Bible?

In the past God spoke to our ancestors through the prophets at many times and in various ways, but in these last days he has spoken to us by his Son, whom he appointed heir of all things, and through whom also he made the universe.

Hebrews 1:1–2

Chapter 3

Inkblots and Puzzles

How, Then, Are We Reading?

In the 1990s, Kris heard about a new kind of book called *Magic Eye*, and she bought one for our kids for Christmas. Perhaps you remember the popularity of *Magic Eye* books. Whether you do or don't, I hope you can find one somewhere and open it up and look at its pictures, which really aren't pictures. They are autostereograms. The pictures in these books, if we let our eyes do what they can do, somehow transform from normal two-dimensional images into three-dimensional images. In front of you is what appears to be a flat picture, perhaps with some dots. But, if you look at that picture just right — if you have eyes to see! — what you think is an ordinary picture of dots and an assortment of shapes begins to take on life. We see humans and flowers and planets in the sky in three dimensions. (I have to admit that this is pretty easy for me, and I have been standing where men stand in designated rooms in public buildings and had the wall in front of me, nothing more than ordinary wallpaper, take on 3D!)

What we are looking for in reading the Bible is the ability to turn the two-dimensional words on paper into a three-dimensional encounter with God, so that the text takes on life and meaning and depth and perspective and gives us direction for what to do today. Gaining Magic Eyes ushers us into the renewal way of reading the Bible.

Perhaps another analogy will work. Who of us, once having read C. S. Lewis's *The Voyage of the Dawn Treader*, can forget the scene where Eustace Scrubb and Lucy and Edmund Pevensie stare at a picture on a wall of a Narnian ship when suddenly the picture draws them into a whole new world? Suddenly that picture on the wall comes alive and they begin to feel the breeze, smell the air, and hear sounds. The kids are magically drawn into the painting and find themselves in the water, where they are helped into a boat with the enticing name *The Dawn Treader*. These kids, now in a new reality, travel to distant lands looking for the seven lost lords of Narnia. At the end of their adventures they find a lamb that turns into Aslan. Great story.

It is that sort of adventure with the Bible that we are looking for, the adventure of staring at the Bible's words on paper only to find ourselves drawn into the story itself. We feel it, taste it, hear it, and come to know it with such perspective and depth that it renews us. That kind of renewal gives us courage to begin living it all over again in our world, but in a new way for a new day. This is the way of renewal.

No Shortcuts!

We find our Magic Eyes and we are drawn up onto *The Dawn Treader* only *when we learn to read the Bible as a story*. The Bible's story, in the simplest of categories, has a plot with a:

> Beginning (Genesis 1 – 11), and a (long, long)
> Middle (Genesis 12 – Malachi 4; Matthew – Revelation), and an
> End (Matthew 25; Romans 8; Revelation 21 – 22).

I am tempted to dive right now into this story, to show that reading every passage in the Bible in light of the story draws us into the story. But we first have to point out some shortcuts too many of us have been taking. In our next chapter will we begin to look at the story of the Bible and its plot.

I wish I could explain it all but I can't. Somewhere we've gone astray and we've stopped reading the Bible as story. Our intent, and it is the right one, is to get something out of the Bible for our daily lives. I too want the Bible to be a "light for my path" (Psalm 119:105) and I'm sure you do as well. But, because reading the Bible as story takes more time, thinking, and discerning, we've developed routines and techniques that get us to our goal sooner. We've learned the CliffsNotes version of the Bible, or we settle for a brief synopsis; we've developed shortcuts to grace. In my years of teaching the Bible, I've found five shortcuts to grace from listening to students and church folk who reveal how they read the Bible in the questions they ask.

One of my son's good friends, Kevin Patterson, is short and a little heftier than he'd like to be. Kevin, like a cairn terrier, is always up for a new challenge. Several years ago, Kevin acquired a new desire to work on his body, but the old-fashioned way of running and lifting and sit-ups wasn't working for him, so he decided that Ab Tronic was the answer. Caught in the lure of a TV ad, Kevin became convinced that if he bought this contraption, a device that fit around his belly and sent short electronic impulses to contract his muscles, he'd lose weight. The rationale given was impeccable: "It's that easy and thirty minutes daily is usually all it takes to help improve figure problems." (So says the Internet ad.) Here's the pillow promise: "Muscles can be shaped while you are reading, relaxing, walking, or doing housework." Ergo, buy the thing!

So, for about a month, whenever Kevin came by (to play on our son's Xbox), he wore his Ab Tronic device. After all, it said it "tones and tightens your upper abs, lower abs, and love handles with no sweat at all." The picture of a well-toned man in his mind didn't hurt. "Say good-bye to strenuous, time-consuming workouts. With the Ab Tronic, your muscles are moving but you are not." Just what Kevin wanted—he could play XBox and lose weight. We've since learned that these devices don't accomplish what they say they will. Kevin will fess up that it didn't work.

Here's my point: many of us, instead of taking the longer but more rewarding path of reading the Bible as story, want a shortcut, an Ab Tronic approach to Bible reading. We want to get the benefits—a toned body—without the effort of working out. We want the electronic impulse of contact with God and grace for the day without the effort of exercising our minds by reading the Bible and discerning how it all fits together and how we can live it out in our day in our way. Just as shortcuts in exercise prevent full health benefits, so also *shortcuts in Bible reading affect our spiritual health.*

Here are a few I've observed:

SHORTCUT 1: *Morsels of Law*

For some, the Bible is massive collection of laws—what to do and what not to do. It is not difficult to understand how the Bible, which contains plenty of commandments and prohibitions—there are 613 in the Old Testament alone—can gradually take on the impression that it is a collection of legal morsels, a law book. Nor is it an uncommon experience, especially for the younger generation, to express the sentiment that "law book" is how they were taught the Bible, and it turned them off to the Bible.

Why? It begins with God. God becomes the Law-God, usually a little ticked off and impatient. Our relationship to God becomes conditioned by whether we are good citizens. There's another ugly element to the mistake of making the Bible a law book: what it does to us. We, the Obedient Ones, become insufferable. How so? We ...

> become intoxicated with our own moral superiority.
> become more concerned with being right than being good.
> become judgmental.

In short, law book readers become pompous, self-righteous, and accusatory. Sometimes we become resentful that others haven't caught up to our level of holiness. I use "we" because I, like the Delphic oracle, know whereof I speak.

I was a teenage legalist and considered myself one of the Obedient Ones. We happily tossed away a few of the Bible's commands, like loving our enemies, because we were crusaders and zealots for wholehearted obedience to the commands of God. In their place we added more commandments, and the ones that particularly appealed to me were "thou shalt not dance," "thou shalt not go to movies," "thou shalt not drink," and "thou shalt not play cards (except Rook or Dutch Blitz)." (God was still uttering his timeless commands in King James English in the sixties and seventies, at least he did in my church.) It was these "thou shalt nots" that made me particularly righteous because it convinced me, in front of God and the whole world, that I had joined an elite fraternity of the faithful. I could go on, but you probably get the picture.

There is, of course, an important place for the Bible's laws, commandments, and prohibitions. If you read Psalm 119 in one sitting, which is possible even if difficult, you will encounter an ancient Israelite who found utter delight in the Lawgiver. You will find a psalmist who loved God. You will find a man (I assume) who didn't see laws as a burden but as the good revelation of God on how to walk in this world with God in such a way that it would lead to the blessing of God. Yes, commandments aplenty can be found in the Bible.

But converting the story of the Bible, and we'll get to this in the next chapter, into a collection of little more than commandments completely distorts the Bible. We need to move on.

Shortcut 2: *Morsels of Blessings and Promises*

In 1551 a certain Stephanus divided the New Testament up into numbered verses. We are thankful (with some groans). Thankful, because now it is much easier to refer to a specific part of the Bible. It is easier to say "John 1:14" than to say "That line in the Bible where it says 'The Word became flesh.'" Numbering verses is one thing, but when publishers provide a Bible where the only divisions are chapters and verses, as if each verse were a new paragraph, reading the Bible as a story is much more difficult. Take your favorite novel or book, photocopy a page, cut out each sentence, number each sentence, and then paste them back onto a page with each number beginning at the left margin, and you'll see the problem. It's much harder to read a book that way. One has to wonder what got into the head of publishers who started doing this. It's a colossal mistake.

Even more importantly, we need to observe what versification did to how we read the Bible. Dividing the Bible up into verses turns the Bible into morsels and leads us to *read the Bible as a collection of divine morsels, sanctified morsels of truth.* We pause for each one to see if we can get something from it. Now I want to meddle with a significant problem. For some morsel readers of the Bible, the Bible has become a collection of morsels of *blessings*, and we can write one out for each day of the week.

> On Monday we get Psalm 23:1
> On Tuesday we get Matthew 5:3
> On Wednesday we get Luke 11:2
> On Thursday we get Jeremiah 31:31
> On Friday we get Mark 14:24
> On Saturday we get Matthew 11:28
> On Sunday we get Romans 4:25

Random verses, with generosity poured on top of generosity. On other calendars we get, instead of a blessing, a *promise* each day — promises about

> God's faithfulness
> God's grace
> God's power
> God's love
> God's patience
> God's listening to our prayers
> God's eternal plans for us

Random verses, with blessing on top of blessing or promise on top of promise. (No one has yet composed a Wrath of God Calendar of Warnings, though some seem poised to begin making such a calendar.)

What happens to the Christian who reads the Bible, day after day and week after week, as little more than a collection of morsels of blessings and promises? (You might want to sit down with a friend and talk about this.) For one, everything is good and wonderful and light and airy. These people become optimistic and upbeat and wear big smiles … *until* something bad happens, until they enter into a period of suffering and feel distant from God, or until they hit a wall. For every hill, there is a valley.

One of the most important things about the Bible is that it tells realistic truth. Sure, there are all kinds of wonderful blessings surrounding Abraham, Moses, David, and Paul … and there also days of doubt, defeat, disobedience, and darkness. David was on top of the world at times, but he also asked God this question: "My God, my God, why have you forsaken me?" (Psalm 22:1). Edith Humphrey, a New Testament scholar, made this important observation of what happens when we focus solely on blessings and promises: "It is unfortunately the case that some contemporary expressions of Christianity have forgotten, or are embarrassed by, this moment of dark reflection, and instead espouse an unrealistic and warped view of spiritual victory." She also speaks of the "relentlessly upbeat" moods that lead to "false security and canned joy."[1]

It is important to know the blessings and to rely on God's promises. Please don't misunderstand my point. But the blessings and promises of God in the Bible emerge from a real life's story that also knows that we live in a broken world and some days are tough. The stories of real lives in the Bible know that we are surrounded by hurting people for whom Psalm 22:1 echoes their normal day.

Those who read the Bible as story refuse to cut up the Bible into morsels of blessings and promises because they know the Story. They know that the David who found God's blessing and trusted in God's promises knew the dark side of life. Imagine how the God of the universe, who chose for some reason to communicate with us in the very thing that makes humans so distinct—sophisticated language in the form of a story covering spans of time—must respond as he observes his people seeking random sayings! It's a wonder that God hasn't at some point made the words disappear from the page, so that we open our Bibles up and nothing but blank paper stares us in the face.[2] We deserve it.

SHORTCUT 3: Mirrors and Inkblots

Hermann Rorschach (1884–1922), a famous Swiss Freudian psychiatrist, devised the inkblot test, and you've probably seen one. What happens is quite straightforward: you (the patient) are shown a card on which one sees an inkblot; you tell the therapist that you see, say, a butterfly; and the therapist—with that special Mona Lisa smile—thinks to herself: "This person's normal." But if you say, "I see my neighbor's brain" or if you start mentioning a pelvis, the therapist—with that same Mona Lisa smile—begins to think in terms of deviancy and disorders. What a person sees in the inkblot gives the therapist information about a person's personality, emotions, and thought processes. It doesn't matter what the inkblot is—it really isn't anything. It gives a person an opportunity to reveal himself or herself.

Some people read the Bible as if its passages were Rorschach inkblots. They see what is in their head. In more sophisticated language, they project onto the Bible what they want to see. If you show them enough passages and you get them to talk about them, you will hear what is important to *them*, whether it is in the Bible or not! They might see in the "Jesus inkblot" a Republican or a socialist, because they are Republicans or socialists. Or, they may see in the book of Revelation, a favorite of inkblot readers, a sketch of contemporary international strife. Or, they may have discovered in the inkblot called "Paul" a wonderful pattern for how to run a church, which just happens to be the pastor's next big plan! You get the point—reading the Bible as an inkblot is projecting onto the Bible *our* ideas and *our* desires.

I give students a test each semester in my Jesus class on opening day.

(The test can be found at Appendix 2 at the end of the book.) That test asks them to fill out a basic personality questionnaire about their view of Jesus and then to answer the same questions, now slightly shifted, about themselves. The amazing result, and the test has been field-tested by some professionals, is that *everyone thinks Jesus is like them!* The test results also suggest that, even though we like to think we are becoming more like Jesus, the reverse is probably more the case: *we try to make Jesus like ourselves.* Which means, to one degree or another, we are all Rorschachers; we all project onto Jesus our own image.[3]

Hardly a month goes by that I don't get an advertisement about a new book. Inevitably, the marketing department gives me the same song and dance: "Here, for the first time, we see what Jesus was really like. Here, for the first time, we get back to Jesus as he really was." Studies about Jesus are my professional specialization and I am willing to say this: Anyone who says they are about to reveal what Jesus was really like is about to reveal not what Jesus was like, but *what they are like.* They've used Jesus as a Rorschach inkblot. You can count on it. I could list the books.

Instead of being swept into the Bible's story, Rorschach thinkers sweep the Bible up into their own story. Instead of being an opportunity for redemption, the Bible becomes an opportunity for narcissism. This is the problem with taking this shortcut: reading the Bible becomes patting ourselves on the back and finding our story in the Bible, instead of finding the Bible's story to be our story. Instead of entering into that story, we manipulate the story so it enters into our story.

I want to turn now to a different kind of shortcut, a hard-earned shortcut that also makes us rethink how we read the Bible.

Shortcut 4: Puzzling Together the Pieces to Map God's Mind

For some people the Bible is like a big puzzle. Once you've got the puzzle solved, you no longer have to work with the pieces. The shortcut is that once you've expended the energy to solve the puzzle, the job is done—forever and a day. These people know what the Bible says before they open it up because they've already puzzled it together.

One of the English translations sitting on my desk has 1,153 pages. Spread over those 1,153 pages, in random order and with no clear clues as to where to begin or which pieces of information are most important, are Bible verses that contain information like pieces in a puzzle. God has scattered his mind throughout the Bible, and he gives to us, his readers, the challenge of putting the puzzle together. Puzzlers belong to what I call the Flat Bible Society. They work in a flat room, and they've scattered throughout the room these random puzzle bits of information from the Bible. If you pick up the right piece first and gradually work your way through every verse (the pieces of the puzzle) of the whole Bible, you will eventually get your Bible's puzzle pieces to look like the picture on the box … but that's the problem. We don't really know what the picture looks like. We have to *imagine* what the original picture was.

Truth be told, this kind of pieced-together puzzle, the Grand System that we construct out of the pieces, is an act of theological imagination. And you know what Mark Twain said about "imagination"? Speaking of Captain Stormfield, he said, "He had a good deal of imagination, and it probably colored his statements of fact; but if this was so, he was not aware of it."[4] Too many puzzlers don't know that the puzzle they believe in is an imagined system of thought.

What's wrong with this shortcut? First, *we need to think about what this Grand System, the solved puzzle, really is*: it is a system of thought that presumes that we know what God was doing behind the Bible before the Bible was written, and once we have this puzzle in hand we've got the Bible figured out. At some level, these folks think they have *mapped the mind of God*. Their map, or their solved puzzle, is something no author in the Bible believes. Instead, the solved puzzle is something God was revealing over time that they have put together. While we don't often think like this, the enormity of this claim boggles the mind (or it should).

Second, this approach nearly always *ignores the parts of the puzzle that don't fit.* Some evening, sit down with an encyclopedia and read the entries on the major groups in the church—Roman Catholics, Eastern Orthodox, Lutherans, Reformed, Congregationalists, Baptists, Episcopalians, Presbyterians, nondenominational, and so on. What you will undoubtedly see is that each one of these groups emphasizes something true and important in the Bible; you will also see that each one de-emphasizes or even ignores something important to the other groups. Each of these groups has a solved puzzle that guides their thinking—no one's puzzle is complete, no one's puzzle is perfect. Each of these groups ignores parts of the puzzle that don't quite fit their system.

Third, *puzzling together the pieces we find in the Bible into a system is impossible.* The Bible contains authors as diverse as Moses and David (who hardly ever quotes Moses), Isaiah and Ezekiel, Daniel and Matthew, John and Paul, Peter and James, as well as Hebrews and Luke. I have sometimes puzzled pieces from all over the Bible together in what I thought were clever, creative, and meaningful ways. Just as often, I have had a pit in my stomach with this worry: my puzzle is not the puzzle of anyone's in the Bible. It is *my* puzzle, not the Bible's.

Think about it this way: it is one thing to pull together the social thinking of Charles Dickens from his novels, and many would say that can be more or less accomplished. But now let's expand our efforts to include other novelists: Why in the world would we even try to pull together the social thinking of all nineteenth-century English novelists? This is not unlike what puzzlers are doing with the various authors of the Bible. Then why do we try to pull together all the authors of the Bible? Who ever told us that was the way to read the Bible? Some might say, "But the Bible is a unity because God is behind it all." I agree, but who says that our system is that unity? Our next concern might shed some light on that question for you; I know it does for me.

Fourth, puzzling *calls into question the Bible as we have it.* After all, had he wanted to, God could have revealed a systematic theology chapter by chapter. But God didn't choose this way of revealing his truth. Maybe—this "maybe" is a little facetious—that way of telling the truth can't tell it the way God wants his truth told. What God chose to do was to give to you and me a story of Israel and the church, and we have a series of authors who tell that story and who contribute in one way or another to that story as the plot unfolds.

So, and here I anticipate something later in the book, maybe we should follow God's design and let the Bible be the Bible. What does that mean? Maybe it is the *story* of the Bible that is the system! No one has spoken more timely words here than Eugene Peterson:

> The most frequent way we have of getting rid of the puzzling or unpleasant difficulties in the Bible is to systematize it, organizing it according to some scheme or other that summarizes "what the Bible teaches." If we know what the Bible teaches, we don't have to read it anymore, don't have to enter the story and immerse ourselves in the odd and unflattering and uncongenial way in which this story develops, including so many people and circumstances that have nothing to do, we think, with us.[5]

What is the problem here? In one word, *mastery*. Those who solve the puzzle think they've got the Bible mastered; they have caged and tamed the Blue Parakeet who gave us the blue parakeets. God did not give the Bible so we could master him or it; God gave the Bible so we could live it, so we could be mastered by it. The moment we think we've mastered it, we have failed to be readers of the Bible. Of course, I think we should read the Bible and know it—but it is the specific element of reading for mastery versus reading to be mastered that grows out of this shortcut.

Now I present a final shortcut, a tasty but tempting one.

Shortcut 5: *Maestros*

I like to cook, and I consider myself an amateur specialist in making risotto, an Italian way of making rice. Kris and I recently spent a week in Italy on vacation, and I ate risotto every evening, sampling the recipe of each cook's way of making risotto. My intent was to see how a *maestro di cucina*, a master of the art of Italian cooking, makes risotto so I could improve my own risotto. In Stresa, near Lago Maggiore on the northern tip of Italy, we went to Hotel Ristorante Fiorentino. Carla Bolongaro welcomed, seated, and served us while her son, Luigino, the *maestro di cucina*, prepared our dinner. ("Dinner" seems hollow for what an Italian cook offers.) All risottos are prepared in thick-bottomed pans, the starches of the rice drawn out from the Carnaroli or Arborio rice with broth one ladle at a time. Luigino added saffron and some tasty prosciutto along with some bits of porcini mushroom (*mama mia!*). By the time we left we knew we had tasted risotto at its finest.

I don't tell you this to make you hungry, or to mention that I have several times done my best to imitate the risotto recipe of the Bolongaro family, but to say that many read the Bible the way they learn from a *maestro di cucina*. That is, they go to the Bible to find the master, the *über*-Rabbi — Jesus — at work. Then, when they get up from their reading of the Bible, they imitate Maestro Jesus. "What would Jesus do?" is the only question they ask. The problem here is the word "only."

It is almost justifiable to make Jesus the Maestro. But more than a few of us are aware that Jesus has been eclipsed by many Bible readers by Maestro Paul. In this shortcut, Jesus is either ignored or overwhelmed by Paul's way of thinking. Some of us grew up in churches where the thought patterns, the lenses, the grid through which everything was filtered — however unconsciously — was the book of Romans or Paul's theology.

I'm one such person. I grew up in a Pauline world and I went to a college and studied Bible in a Pauline world. Even when we dipped into the Gospels, especially at Christmas and Easter, we used Maestro Paul to inform us about what Jesus was really doing and saying. I cannot tell you what it was like when, as a first-year seminary student, I sat under Walt Liefeld and listened — at 7:45 a.m. — with my jaw agape — to someone who could open the world of Jesus for me. Right then and there, in the deepest recesses of my soul, I knew I had found my life's passion—to study and teach about Jesus. I had been tutored under Maestro Paul and found Jesus.

The problem was not Paul. (I'll get to that soon enough.) The problem was that I was not taught to read the Bible as a story and many of us weren't. I had been nurtured in a world that read the entire Bible as a solved puzzle that used Maestro Paul's categories to understand everything else in the Bible. Reading the Bible through a maestro's eyes gives us one chapter in the story of the Bible. One-chapter Bible readers develop one-chapter Christian lives.

Now that I've pointed out some shortcuts we all too often take, what is the long way? How can we learn to read the Bible as Story? How can we develop Magic Eyes and be drawn up onto *The Dawn Treader*? As the guide at the museum says as she moves onto the next room, "Step this way."

Chapter 4

It's a Story with Power!

How, Then, Shall We Read?

Blogging may be the world's most fascinating form of communication. Someone jots down their ideas, clicks "publish," and those ideas instantaneously appear for the whole world to see. The world does see. More importantly, the world sometimes comments back. Sometimes anonymously and sometimes bitingly and sometimes it hurts. The first lesson a blogger learns is this: anyone in the world can say anything they want at anytime on a blog. The second lesson is this: you may not know that person. In my first week of blogging at www.jesuscreed.org I learned these two lessons, and they shocked me. One of the first questions that wandered its way through my head when I began reading a comment on something I had written was: "Who is this person anyway?"

After years of teaching, preaching, and writing, comments and questions were common for me. I am used to being questioned. In fact, I enjoy it. But teachers know who is saying what and more often than not we also know where our students' questions are "coming from." But those who drop comments in the comment box on a blog can do so anonymously or with a fictitious name. Under the cloak of anonymity, they can become bold and brazen and can blast away. Incivility marks blogs far too often. To be sure, blogs form blog communities where most learn enough about other commenters that, even if we don't know the person personally, we recognize their electronic personality. Knowing one another restores civility. Still, until one discovers "who is who" and "where they are coming from," comments can sometimes startle and shock.

On my blog we have developed a simple protocol: no anonymous comments. Why? Since I believe "context is everything," context-less comments and faceless comments, which are what fictitious names or anonymous comments are, are not permitted. Anyone who speaks up anonymously or fictitiously is context-less. Until we know the context or until we know who is saying what and why, it is difficult to know how to respond.

Reading the Bible is the same: context is everything. Until we learn to read each text in its context, we run the risk of misunderstanding the Bible. I'll give an example. Do you pay interest on your loans? Do you participate in (or with) a company that charges interest? The Bible says some clear things about charging interest in Leviticus 25:35–38:

> If any of your own people become poor and are unable to support themselves among you, help them as you would a foreigner and stranger, so they can continue to live among you. Do not take interest or any profit from them, but fear your God, so that your poor neighbors may continue to live among you. You must not lend them money at interest or sell them food at a profit. I am the LORD your God, who brought you out of Egypt to give you the land of Canaan and to be your God.

It's about as clear as the lenses on my glasses (which for some obsessive reason I keep clean). But, and I'm willing to bet on this one, none of us obeys this commandment. Interest was prohibited, full stop, no questions asked. God put his reputation on the line for this one. (That's the point of last verse quoted above.) Now you might start fiddling around and say that since it was for fellow Israelites, this means only we shouldn't charge interest or pay interest to fellow Christians. This only pushes us further into the corner, because—and I'm willing to bet on this one too—we don't bother to check up on our mortgages to make sure Christians aren't charging interest to us. Besides, the effort it would require, we don't care because we aren't interested in this commandment in the Bible. Why is this? It all has to do with how you and I read our Bibles.

You probably read this prohibition of interest the way I do: *that was then, and this is now.* Reading the Bible like this is reading the Bible as Story. It unfolds and propels us to live out the Bible in our day in our way. But how do we know when the principle of "that was then and this is now" applies? It's easy when everyone agrees, and we all seem to have concluded without much conscious effort—though we'd all be surprised how debated interest was in Europe in centuries past—that charging and paying interest is how the system works. But what happens when some disagree with the status quo? It's not so easy then. When some disagree, we suddenly notice the blue parakeet in our presence and begin to rethink how we read the Bible.

I believe those seven words are the secret to reading the Bible: "that was then and this is now." They reveal that we have learned to read the Bible as Story, even though most of us never give this a minute's thought. We need to. That is why this first section of the book, devoted to "the Story," needs to be given the attention we give it. Until we learn to read the Bible as Story, we will not know how to get anything out of the Bible for daily living. We will not become aware how we can so easily dispense with what the Bible says about interest. And, unless we read the Bible as Story, we might be tempted to make "that was then" into "it's also now." But it isn't. Times have changed. God spoke in Moses' days in Moses' ways (about interest), and he spoke in Jesus' days in Jesus' ways, and he spoke in Paul's days in Paul's ways. *And he speaks in our days in our ways*—and it is our responsibility to live out what the Bible says in our days. We do this by going back so we can come forward.

It's a Story!

As we go back to the Bible, we ask a big question: How would you classify and shelve the Bible in a library? Using the Dewey Decimal System, where would you put it? Since the architects of the DDS have already assigned it to Religion (200), where it has its own number (Bible — 200), the answer to our question might seem easy. But, if we think about how people treat or read the Bible, and we think back to our third chapter where we talked about shortcuts, we might find ourselves in an interesting conversation. It seems to me that here is where some folks would shelve the Bible in a library:

Lawbook:	320 (Political science) → 340 (Law)
Blessings/promises for the day:	150 (Psychology) → 158 (Applied)
Rorschach:	158 (Applied psychology) or 126 (The self)
Puzzle:	110 (Metaphysics) or 120 (Epistemology)
Maestro:	227.06 (Paul) or 232.092 (Jesus Christ)

Each of these locations on the shelves of the library tells us something true about the Bible. In fact, it is amazing how many locations could contain Bibles! Apart from its obvious location with Religion, the Bible properly belongs with History of the Ancient World, Palestine/Israel (933), and also in the Life of Jesus (232.092); and because the gospel spreads from the land of Israel throughout the whole world, it could also be moved to World History (909). But there's one element about the Bible that makes the DDS inadequate: the Bible claims to be God's telling of history. The Bible is the story of God's people. It is "*his*" story, and I doubt any library wants to assign a number to "God's Story"!

Going back to the Bible teaches us to read the Bible as God's story. Read, as an example, Acts 7. Here we have someone who puts the whole Bible together for us. Stephen, an early Christian deacon, was about to be put to death for following Jesus. The future apostle Paul (then called

Saul) chimed in with his judgment and approved the capital sentence for Stephen.

But first Stephen was put on trial. He was asked if the charges against him were true. Stephen's answer is an example of how to read the Bible. He didn't do anything other than tell the story of Israel that had opened a new chapter—a chapter called Jesus the Messiah. With Jesus, everything changed. Everything! Stephen had to follow Jesus even if meant dying for him. If you follow along with Stephen's story, you are sucked into the Story, just as the Pevensie kids were drawn into the picture and onto *The Dawn Treader*. If you are looking for an argument, a kind of "point one, point two, point three, therefore do this," you may not find your Magic Eyes in Acts 7. It's there for those with eyes to see.

All across the spectrum today experts are also saying we need to read the Bible as Story. Robert Webber, a wonderfully influential and now deceased Wheaton professor, offers us an invitation: "So I invite you to read the Bible," he said, "not for bits and pieces of dry information [pieces in a puzzle], but as the story of God's embrace of the world told in poetic images and types."[1] I add another voice, namely, the excellent Old Testament scholar John Goldingay: "The biblical gospel is not a collection of timeless statements such as God is love. It is a narrative about things God has done."[2] For a third voice, consider a Jewish scholar, Abraham Joshua Heschel: "The God of the philosopher is a concept derived from abstract ideas; the God of the prophets is derived from acts and events. The root of Jewish faith is, therefore, not a comprehension of abstract principles but an inner *attachment to those events*."[3]

Each of these scholars points us in the same direction. In your hand is a Bible that God gave you to read. God asks us to read the Bible as the unfolding of the story of his ways to his people. Stephen was killed for telling that story.

So was William Tyndale. Tyndale was put to death because he wanted to make a reality the Reformation's most dangerous idea[4]—putting the Bible and its powerful story in the hands of every Christian so each of us could read it. The Bible in your hand is there because of William Tyndale. You may not know what a privilege it is. For most of the first 1,500 years of the church, the average person did not have a Bible, and even if they did, most could not read. Tyndale was the vanguard for English translations.

I want to pause here to pay homage to one of our greatest Bible translators, because we need to be reminded that the Bible I am writing about in this book, the Bible that you and I hold in our hands, is a Bible that cost some people their lives just to translate.

William Tyndale
Gives Us the Bible

I am surrounded by books and Bibles. Most of us read the Bible in English; I have a number of translations, and you probably do too. The roots of all English translations go back to William Tyndale.[5] Tyndale had a goal in life: "If God spare my life, ere many years I will cause a boy that driveth the plough shall know more of the Scripture than thou [a learned man] dost." His goal? To translate the whole Bible so clearly that even farm boys could read and understand it.

The Roman Catholic establishment of England was opposed to translating the Bible for fear that what was happening in Germany, namely, the explosive Reformation led by Martin Luther, might come to England. What was there to fear? The Bible. Nothing but the Bible. The clergy's knowledge of the Bible at that time would shock the reader today. Some did not know which book of the Bible contained the Ten Commandments (many thought they were found in Matthew's gospel), some did not know where to find the Lord's Prayer (which was said constantly in Catholic services), some did not know who originally said it, and some could not even recite it. Tyndale's dream ran headfirst against the establishment. What Luther had done in Germany was about to land in England.

Tyndale began work on a translation of the Bible into plain English but could not find support for his work in England, so he crossed the English Channel to Germany, hoping to be carried by Luther's steam. In Cologne, Germany, in 1525, as Tyndale was translating Matthew 22 (he was on verse 12), he and his companion William Roye escaped an attempt to arrest and imprison them for their supposedly seditious work of translating the Bible.

Five years later, a certain Thomas Hitton was arrested in England for preaching heresy. "At his examination he confessed that he had smuggled a New Testament ... from abroad. After imprisonment he was condemned ... and on 23 February burned alive at Maidstone." The religious establishment meant business when they prohibited translation.

Tyndale translated most of the Bible, but before he was finished he was tricked "by a vicious, paltry and mean villain" who revealed Tyndale's location. In October of 1536, Tyndale was tied to the stake and strangled by an executioner. His last words were an expression of nothing less than his simple vision to translate the Bible into plain English: "Lord! Open the king of England's eyes!" We wonder if the crowd behind the barricade that watched the gathering of brushwood and straw and which stepped aside to watch Tyndale mount the place of execution heard his prayer. Did they hear what he said when the authorities asked him that last time to recant his stubborn ways? They would have seen him tied to a stake and the rope gathered around his neck. After signaling that it was time to tighten the rope and letting it do what it was designed to do, the authorities judged him dead. They set the kindling afire to consume the body of a man who had but one goal—to make the Bible readable for everyone.

You and I have a Bible, and most of us read it without fear. To quote Augustine, *tolle lege*: "take, read." As Tyndale's biographer said it, "The bare text [of the Bible], if given whole, will interpret itself." But we must read it—and that means from Genesis to Revelation—as it is meant to be read.

A Confession

For many years, instead of grasping the Bible as Story, I was a Maestro Bible reader. I learned to tame the blue parakeets—and there were plenty in the Bible to tame—by making them all sound like Maestro Jesus, the *über*-Rabbi. At times I sneaked into the cabins of others for a meal or two with other cooks; that is, I wrote commentaries on Galatians and 1 Peter. During this time I nursed a grudge against two authors who, for me, were blue parakeets: the apostle Paul and the apostle John. Why? I believed they had *ignored* the kingdom message of Jesus.

I was upset with Paul and Peter for using words like "justification" and "church" and "eternal life"—not that there is anything wrong with their terms. So devoted was I to the Maestro's verbal vision that I thought these other New Testament writers should have used Jesus' pet expression, namely, "kingdom of God." I could not understand why Paul dropped terms like "disciple" or why he seemed to ignore the Sermon on the Mount or why John translated "kingdom" into "eternal life." So I tamed them by using only Jesus' words.

Furthermore, as a Maestro reader of the Bible I also nursed a grudge against the puzzlers of this world, and my grudge emerged from two convictions about how to read the Bible. First (and I still sense this at times), those who have a solved puzzle rarely let Jesus' kingdom message be what it is. Second, every approach I've read by puzzlers somehow managed to avoid the Story and the Plot as the central categories for knowing the message of the Bible. Instead of creation and fall, exodus and exile, as well as community and redemption, the Story was flattened out. Categories like God, man, Christ, sin, salvation, and eschatology were pieced together from various authors. Unfortunately, the authors themselves were not given their day before the jury. I congratulated myself for being hyperbiblical about Jesus' message of the kingdom, which I thought was better than the puzzling approach. But while I was fair to Jesus, I didn't have an approach that let each author in the Bible tell their own story.

But that all changed when I realized that God chose to communicate with us in language. This may seem either profoundly obvious, on the level of the person who says the sky is above us, or "profoundly profound." For me this was profoundly profound. Since—and this is why it changed how I read the Bible—God chose to communicate in language, since language is always shaped by context, and since God chose to speak to us over time through many writers, God also chose to speak to us in a variety of ways and expressions. Furthermore, I believe that because the gospel story is so deep and wide, *God needed a variety of expressions to give us a fuller picture of the Story.*

This liberated me from the Maestro approach and drove me to the Story approach of reading the Bible. I now know that the various versions of the Story in the Bible need to be seen for what they are: "wiki"-stories of the Story. (I'll get to this "wiki" idea if you'll read one more paragraph.)

In our Bible, God did what God has always done: he spoke in Moses' days in Moses' ways, in Micah's days in Micah's ways, and in Jesus' days in Jesus' ways. Which meant, when Paul came around, Paul got to speak in Paul's ways for Paul's days, and when John put quill to parchment, he was freed up to speak in John's ways for John's days. This discovery liberated me, and (to use some puns now, so catch them) it justified Paul and gave new life to John to take Jesus' kingdom story and make it their own story of the Story. I've come to see these stories of the Story to be like the seventh day of creation—very, very good. No single story, not even Jesus' story, can tell the whole Story. We need them all.

Why Wiki-Story?

So, you ask, why see the various authors as "wiki" stories? Most of us are familiar with Wikipedia. Those who say they aren't will be sentenced to read Karl Barth's *Church Dogmatics* for ten consecutive hours for not telling the truth! Wikipedia has its detractors and its problems, but that won't keep the world or our students (or any of us) from using it. It is a collaborative, democratic, interactive, developing encyclopedia to which anyone in the world, ostensibly, can make a contribution.

Wikipedia is not like your father's encyclopedia, whether that was *World Book* or *Britannica*. Instead, an entry in Wikipedia can change daily: paragraphs can be deleted and entries can be completely rewritten or new entries added. It's sometimes called "open source." (Here's the path to the Wikipedia entry for "Open Source": http://en.wikipedia.org/wiki/Open_source.) Because it is truly "open," bad information can filter into the entries and render their quality suspect. In calling the Bible a Wiki-Story I will bracket off the problems of bad contributors to Wikipedia. All I want to focus on here is one element: *the ongoing reworking of the biblical Story by new authors so they can speak the old story in new ways for their day.*

If you'd like a more Jewish way of saying each author is a writer of a wiki-story, I'd say the Bible contains an ongoing series of *midrashes*, or interpretive retellings, of the one Story God wants us to know and hear. Each biblical author, whether we talk of Moses and the Pentateuch, or the so-called Deuteronomic histories, or the Chronicler, Job, or Ecclesiastes, or the various prophets, or Jesus or Paul or John or James or the author of Hebrews or Peter—each of these authors tells his version of the Story. They tell wiki-stories of the Story; they give midrashes on the previous stories. Sometimes one author will pick up the story of someone else, as when the Chronicler picks up 1 and 2 Kings, and will recast it, or when Isaiah picks up Micah and Hosea. But other times we have more or less a new story, as with Daniel or Jeremiah or Ezekiel or the apostle Paul or the writer of Hebrews.

If you'd like to see this process in action, open up your Bible to Matthew 4:1–11, Matthew's version of the temptations of Jesus. Matthew here tells a wiki-story, a new version, of an old story. Many— far too many, in fact—have been taught this passage in a blessings/promises or Rorschach approach. They've been taught to read this text for themselves—as a method for responding to temptations to sin. The biblical answer, which is never even remotely mentioned in the text itself, is to quote the Bible at Satan when we are tempted. This makes sense, but it has nothing to do with the text itself.

Here's the question the Story asks us, and it reveals what we mean by a wiki-story: Is Jesus' temptation the reliving of Adam and Eve's experience in Eden? (Jesus is then cast as the Second Adam, only this time perfectly obedient, and thereby the pioneer of a new Adamic line.) Or, which is more probable, is Jesus' temptation by Satan the reliving of Israel's wilderness testings? (Jesus is then recast as the second Moses leading his people to a new Promised Land.) In either case, Matthew casts the story of Jesus' temptations as an updated version, a wiki-story, of an older story—either the Eden story or the wilderness story.

Many New Testament specialists will tell you that nearly every page is a wiki-story on an Old Testament wiki-story. In fact, the Old Testament scholar John Goldingay says the New Testament is nothing but footnotes on the Old Testament![6] He adds that "one cannot produce a theology out of footnotes." That is, if you don't have the Old Testament in your head, you can't grasp what the New Testament authors are saying. (Goldingay, as is typical with him, exaggerates to make a point—only he might not think he's exaggerating.)

Here's where we are:

- The Bible is a Story.
- The Story is made up of a series of wiki-stories.
- The wiki-stories are held together by the Story.
- The only way to make sense of the blue parakeets in the Bible is to set each in the context of the Bible's Story.

None of the wiki-stories is final; none of them is comprehensive; none of them is absolute; none of them is exhaustive. Each of them tells *a true story of that Story*. In our next chapter I want to sketch what the Story looks like.

Chapter 5

The Plot
of the Wiki-Stories

How Does the Bible Work?

S aying the Bible is Story is not saying it is make-believe or a fib or fiction or myth, nor is it to assert that gobs of the stories didn't happen. We say the Bible is Story because if we read it from beginning to end, we discover that it has three features: it has a *plot* (creation to consummation), it has *characters* (God—Father, Son, and Spirit—and God's people and the world and creation around them), and it also has many *authors* who together tell the story. So, to discover the basics of the Story, I will ask you to sit back and imagine something with me.

Imagine Jesus reclining at the head of a table at a writers' banquet. To his right are more than thirty authors, the authors of Old Testament books.[1] To his left are more than ten authors of New Testament books. Each of these authors has his (or her) hand raised—not to ask a question but for permission to tell their story of the Story. Each one has a story to tell, or perhaps even better, each one has *a way* of telling the Story. Before they are given permission, however, Jesus gives them some instructions in the form of a plot to which they are to conform their story. We are only imagining Jesus at the head of this table, of course, and one can find theological reasons to put the Father or the Holy Spirit at the head of the table. Our point is that God directs the Bible along the line of the Story.

Here are the basic elements of the plot to which all Bible writers have been asked to conform, whether or not they choose to bring up each specific element; below we will open up each of these more completely. But for now the elements of the plot in the Story revolve around five themes, which hold the Bible together.

Plot	Theme
Creating *Eikons* (Genesis 1–2)	Oneness
Cracked *Eikons* (Genesis 3–11)	Otherness
Covenant Community (Genesis 12–Malachi)	Otherness expands
Christ, the Perfect *Eikon*, redeems (Matthew–Revelation 20)	One in Christ
Consummation (Revelation 21–22)	Perfectly One

Each author must write their story within this plot, but they are given considerable freedom to tell the Story in their own way. Whether you turn to Exodus or Ezra, Malachi or Mark, or Acts or Hebrews, you must read each book as a variation on this Story.

One of the most exciting features of those who learn to read the Bible as Story is to see how each book or author shapes the various elements of this plot, emphasizing one element or the other. We cannot do this for each book of the Bible in this book, but a good place for you to begin is with one of the minor prophets, say Micah or Haggai, and see what you think each writer does with each of these elements of the plot. Once you get the hang of reading the Bible this way, you can then map the story of each author of the Bible. Before long you will have a notebook full of ideas about each of these points ... but especially the middle ones.

The most important thing I have to say here is this: *The unity of the Bible is this Story. It is this Story that puts the Bible together.* Our grand systems do not form the unity of the Bible; the Story that God tells forms and frames that unity. The plot I sketch below is not simply mine, though I have put my own stamp on it here and there. Essentially, this is the plot the church has always used to understand the narrative flow of the Bible. Recently I read a book called *On the Apostolic Preaching* by a second-century saint, Irenaeus of Lyons (in France). His book is the oldest commentary on how to read the Bible, and the plot I sketch below is essentially the same Irenaeus sketches.[2] It is the only plot the church has ever had.

CREATING *EIKONS*:
Designed for Oneness

We begin at the beginning (Genesis 1 – 2), which begins with God, who creates everything. The instant someone uses the word "create" in the Christian world, however, we face a problem: evolution and creation, faith and science. These debates have made it enormously difficult for modern readers to see what these two chapters are really about. If we drop that concern so we can engage this text, we will discover a window onto the whole Bible.

The pinnacle of God's speaking things into existence was creating human beings. To clarify what God says about this event, I will translate two important words in Genesis 1:26 – 27 with unfamiliar words to grab our attention and lead us to the heart of what creation is all about. "Let us make *The Adam* [human beings] in our own *Eikon* [image, likeness of God]."[3] Here are the verses set out in full:

> Then God said, "Let us make *The Adam* in our *Eikon*, in our likeness, so that they may rule over the fish in the sea and the birds in the sky, over the livestock and all the wild animals, and over all the creatures that move along the ground." So God created *The Adam* in his own *Eikon*, in the *Eikon* of God he created them.

Then the Bible informs us (in Genesis 2) that God chose to "split *The Adam*" into two, into an *Ish* (man) and into an *Ishah* (woman). Thus, Genesis 2:23 reads:

She shall be called *Ishah*, for she was taken out of *Ish*.

The choice to make *The Adam* as an *Eikon* and to split *The Adam* into two, male and female, is profoundly important for understanding the story of the Bible.

The Trinitarian

God creates

↓

The Adam

↓

then splits the lonely *The Adam* into

Ish   in communion with   *Ishah*

and brought together
by God to form

One Flesh

In brief, the point of Genesis 1–2 is this: God wanted *The Adam* to enjoy what the Trinity had eternally enjoyed and what the Trinity continues to enjoy: perfect communion and mutuality with an equal. *The Adam* was in union with God and itself and Eden. But in another sense, *The Adam* stood alone in Genesis 2. As *The Adam* sorts through all the animals, *The Adam* was without communion with an equal. So, to make the need for communion and love abundantly clear, God openly reveals that this aloneness is not what God wants for *The Adam*. God wants *The Adam* to be two in order to experience the glories of communion of love and mutuality.

Several elements in the creation story make the communion-intent of splitting *The Adam* of God clear. Unfortunately, since we've been fighting about creation and evolution for so long, we miss this stuff. The themes of Genesis 1–2 are God's creation of Adam and Eve to enjoy loving mutuality and communion. Notice these elements illustrating that God made Adam and Eve so they could enjoy one another in glorious, loving communion.

- God creates the *Ishah* from the man's rib, from his side, a symbol of companionship and mutuality rather than subordination.
- The *Ishah*, the woman, is called an *ezer kenego*, a companion, in Genesis 2:18: "I will make a helper [companion] suitable for him."
- After splitting *The Adam* into *Ish* and *Ishah*, God brings them back together to become "one flesh." Marriage symbolizes the union of oneness in love. Marriage completes creation. Marriage restores *The Adam* and reveals mutuality.

The creation story is a story of what we were made to be and do:

God is a Trinity, three equal persons in one(ness).
God designs Eikons *for oneness in love.*
God makes The Adam, *who isn't one with an equal.*
So,
God splits The Adam *into two so Adam and Eve can enjoy oneness.*

The relationship of Adam to Eve is like the relation of Father, Son, and Spirit. That is why the Bible says they are "one flesh." This word "one" is the same word used in Israel's famous daily confession, the *Shema*: "Hear, O Israel: The LORD our God, the LORD is *one*" (Deuteronomy 6:4, emphasis added). As God is "one," so Adam and Eve are "one." If you get anything out of Genesis 1–2 this is it:

The loving oneness of God finds earthly expression
in the loving oneness of Adam and Eve.
When Eikons *are at one with God, self, others, and the world,*
the glory of the One God illuminates all of life.

Nothing in the Bible makes sense if one does not begin with the garden of Eden as a life of oneness—human beings in union with God and in communion with the self, with one another, and with the world around them. Life is about "oneness"—oneness with God, with ourselves, with others, and with the world. When this oneness is lived out, God is glorified and humans delight in that glory. This is our Creator's intent, but oneness was about to take a hit in the second element of the Story.

CRACKED *EIKONS*:
Distorting Oneness, Creating Otherness

Mr. and Mrs. *Eikon*, Adam and Eve, in these first two chapters of our Bible are in four oneness relationships: with God, with the self, with one another, and with Eden, the ducky little garden given them to enjoy. But in Genesis 3, Eve, with her husband clearly in tow, chooses to do what God said not to do. As a result, they "crack the *Eikon*" and jeopardize oneness. Again, if we sit down with Genesis 1–3 and forget about evolution, creation, and scientific origins and just read this text for what it says, we learn something profound about who we are and what we are designed to do. What we learn in Genesis 3 is that sin distorts oneness because the Eikon is now cracked.

The first impact of rebelling against God according to the Bible is experienced within the self, in Adam and Eve's self-consciousness. The Bible says they are ashamed of themselves because of their nakedness (3:7; cf. esp. 2:25, "The man and his wife were both naked, and they felt no shame").

The text then continues this march of distorting oneness in that Adam and Eve hide from God and act as if nothing has happened (3:8–9). But, as Mark Twain describes their moral relation to God, "it is very difficult to look as if you have not been doing anything when the facts are the other way."[4]

Third, their oneness with one another shows the impact of sin on their love for one another: they begin to blame each other (3:11–13).

Fourth, to complete the march toward madness, God must open the gates into the real world and send the two cracked *Eikons* east of Eden (3:21–24). The fourfold relationship of oneness, previously enjoyed in the glorious oneness of love, is now completely cracked: they are at odds with God, with self, with one another, and with the world. *Oneness has become otherness.*

Instead of experiencing one another in oneness, they begin to experience one another as "others." In fact, Genesis 3 predicts something that tells the story of human relationships: "Your desire will be for your husband, and he will rule over you" (3:16). This is not a curse as if this *must happen forever and always.* Instead, the desire to rule rises in the human heart because oneness is cracked. Instead of loving one another as they love themselves, they will now desire to climb over the other and on top of the other in order to control and dominate. This fallen story of otherness leads to death.

But the good story of oneness leads to life. *The entire rest of the Bible, aiming as it will toward Jesus Christ, is about turning* Eikons *bent on otherness to* Eikons *basking in oneness with God, with self, with others, and with the world.*

The problem that the fall creates can be called "sin," though that word is not used in Genesis 3. Sin is a cracked relationship of otherness with God, with self, with others, and with the world. The redemptive plan of the Bible is to restore humans into a oneness relationship with God, self, others, and the world. *This otherness problem is what the gospel "fixes," and the story of the Bible is the story of God's people struggling with otherness and searching for oneness.*

COVENANT COMMUNITY:
The Struggle for Oneness

Here too many Bible readers lose their way and jump ahead because they've limited the otherness problem to God and self. Many Christians want to skip from Genesis 3 to the Gospels or Romans 3. Let's remind ourselves of how many of us read the Bible: our plot is creation, fall, and redemption. So, now that we've got the fall, let's get to redemption.

I like this, but there's something missing. (Like 1033 pages!) It is right to see the plot move from creation and fall to redemption, but *how* God chooses to redeem is a giant (three hundred pound!) blue parakeet in the Bible for many readers. The story of the Bible is creation, fall, *and then covenant community*—page after page of community—*as the context* in which our wonderful *redemption* takes place.

If reading the Bible as Story teaches us one thing, it teaches us that it is the *otherness with others* that most concerns God. Otherness of the self and God is the assumption, but otherness with others is the focus of the Story. We in the Western world are obsessed with our individual relationship with God, which leads us to read the Bible as morsels of blessings and promise and as a Rorschach inkblot. But reading the Bible as Story opens up a need so deep we sometimes aren't aware we need it: oneness with others.

Not so fast, God must be saying to the many individualistic Bible readers who want to shake the fall loose by making a beeline to the cross and resurrection. That's not the way God wants us to read the Bible. What does God do after the fall in the Story? God lets his cracked *Eikons* foolishly fiddle around for about seven chapters. At the end of this time God does a do-over with Noah and the flood. Then—and I can't emphasize this enough—God forms a *covenanted community*—a community in which they are to find oneness with God, with self, with *others*, and with the world.

This covenanted community, which focuses on oneness with others, will shape the rest of the Bible. God's idea of redemption is community-shaped. Oneness cannot be achieved just between God and self; rather, oneness involves God, self, *and others, and the world around us.* There are pages and pages about this stuff. If we don't care about how Israel is faring, about how Judah is faring, about kings and prophets and worship centers, or about how Israel longed for the Messiah when oppressed by Rome, we will find the Bible boring indeed. Only after this lengthy set of stories about Israel do we arrive at the New Testament.

Then, in the New Testament, we get the same emphasis as in the Old Testament because we now read about how God's Spirit invaded that little messianic community and drove it out into the Roman Empire — and we are asked to care about how these local communities (i.e., churches) did in the Roman Empire.

Just pick up your Bible and start in Genesis 12 and skim through Esther, some 450 pages in my Bible, and you will observe the story of God's people in the realities of otherness with others and oneness with others. He cares deeply about this — for pages, for centuries. Creation, fall, redemption — yes. But, and here's what so many miss, the *way* God works redemption in this world is *through his covenanted community — first Israel, then the church.*

Otherness Gets the Last Word

But there is a massive problem staring at us as we read this Story: *God's people don't get the job done.* I don't know if this strikes you, but I believe it should: something is terribly wrong with God's covenant people. While there are some high points, like the exodus from Egypt and the return from exile, the people never truly achieve the design God has for them. Here are just a few of the lowlights:

- Only Noah and his family survive the flood and then the man messes things up immediately.
- Abraham is God's chosen father of his people and he lies about his wife.
- Moses murders, rescues Israel at the exodus, gives them the Torah and a worship center, and then sins in the desert.
- Israel gets into the Promised Land but they can't shake off idolatries.
- David is the king and he can't control himself.
- His son builds a great temple but he can't control himself either, so

that within a generation the "oneness" nation becomes a "twoness" nation.

- One of those nations gets deported to Assyria while the other, Judah, hangs on longer but finds itself eventually in Babylon.
- Then God, in his rich mercy, ends the exile and leads Judah back to the Promised Land and they rebuild the temple and ... the whole thing starts all over again. Otherness seemingly gets the last word.

Woven into this story is a deep thread of failure that creates otherness. How to resolve the deep thread of failure drives the story onward. Deep within the fabric of this story is that *Israel won't get the job done until the job is done for them.* That job won't get done until Jesus, Israel's long-awaited Messiah, comes. He will bring the oneness.

CHRIST, THE PERFECT *EIKON*:
Oneness Restored

The Bible's story has a plot headed in the direction of a *person*. And that same story is headed in the direction of a *community* "in" that person.

Everything God designed for *Eikons* is actually lived out by Jesus. Everything *Eikons* are to do comes by being "in Christ" or by becoming "one" with Jesus Christ.

The good gospel things of becoming one with God, self, others, and the world happen to us only *when we are united to Christ, when we become "one" in Christ.* Let me now say this succinctly: The story of the Bible then aims at Galatians 3:28:

> There is neither Jew nor Gentile,
> neither slave nor free,
> neither male nor female,
> for you are all one in Christ Jesus.

The story of the Bible takes the otherness of cracked *Eikons* and directs us toward Jesus Christ, in whom alone we find oneness.

God accomplishes four things in Christ, each of which contributes to the restoration of oneness. These four moments do the job, end the otherness, and create the oneness that the story of the Bible has been yearning for. We need each other; without that, otherness continues to reign; but when the strength of each is tapped into, oneness can be found.

Incarnation

In his *incarnate life*, when he becomes one with us, Jesus recapitulates, or relives, Israel's (our) history. He becomes one of us. In fact, he becomes *all of us* in one divine-human being. Jesus is all Adam and Eve were designed to be, and more; he loves the Father absolutely and he loves himself absolutely and he loves others absolutely and he loves the world absolutely. He is the Oneness Story in one person.

Death

Humans are guilty before God according to Genesis 3; the punishment for that guilt is *death*. Notice how Eve tells the serpent what God had said to her: "You must not eat fruit from the tree that is in the middle of the garden, and you must not touch it, or you will *die*." Otherness leads to death; *the* problem to resolve is death. Thus, because God's intent is to make the *Eikons* what he designed them to be, God takes on our death—our punishment for sin—so that we don't have to die.

God did push Adam and Eve out of the garden of Eden lest they should "live forever" in their "otherness condition." That act of God was an act of mercy—an act that ultimately anticipates the cross of Christ. Jesus' act of dying our death *forgives* us of our complicity in Adam and Eve's sin by assuming what we deserved: death. Three prepositions tell the Story of Jesus' death:

- Jesus dies *with us*—he dies our death and we die with him. He becomes one with our death and we become one with his death.

- Jesus dies *instead of us*—that final death is taken on board by him and we don't have to die that final death.
- Jesus dies *for us*—by assuming our death, we are forgiven of our sin.

But forgiveness is only the beginning of restoring us to oneness.

Resurrection

Eikons, forgiven as they are, are now only in neutral. They are no longer dead. That's not enough. What do humans need? Life. Jesus is raised *for us*. I wish more of us would see how significant the resurrection is for God's redemptive plan, for the story that unfolds in the Bible. By becoming one with the Resurrected One through faith, we are raised to new life. Why? So that we might stand up and walk again as *Eikons* are designed to live—with God, with self, with others, and with the world. The resurrection creates dead *Eikons* walking again.

Pentecost

And now the only need left is the power to create oneness, which is precisely what Pentecost is all about. God sends the promised Spirit of the new covenant so that the covenant community can be empowered to be glowing *Eikons*, people who are restored to oneness with God, self, others, and the world. The most decisive impact of Pentecost, where the gift of the Spirit is made clear, is not tongue-speaking but community-formation (oneness). Read Acts 2.

It is no surprise, then, that Luke's account of Pentecost returns to this theme of oneness. Acts 2:42–47 focuses on the oneness that was achieved now that God's work was finished. "All the believers were together and had everything *in common*" (2:44). Acts 4:32 says this: "All the believers were *one* in heart and mind. No one claimed that any of their possessions was their own, but *they shared everything* they had" (emphasis added in both passages). This is the story the whole Bible was designed to tell: otherness overturned and oneness restored. It happens in the covenant community that is "one" in Christ.

But, again, notice that the focus of this oneness in the Bible is oneness with *others*. Once oneness is restored between God and the self, it begins to work itself out into oneness with others and this world. Love of God is joined with love of others. These words of Paul reveal the plan:

> All this is from God, who reconciled us to himself through Christ and gave us the ministry of reconciliation. (2 Corinthians 5:18)

It's all right here: We (the self) are at one with God, and this leads to oneness (reconciliation) with others in this world.

CONSUMMATION:
Oneness Forever

The Perfect *Eikon's* work, however, is a two-stage work, not unlike the blind man who first saw what he thought were trees and then, once Jesus applied a second dressing of Deep Magic, could see fully. Jesus' first work, the accomplishment of oneness in his first coming, stands now as partial redemption. The fullness of that work, complete union and perfect oneness, when God once again opens the gates to Eden for Adams and Eves, will be consummated only when Christ returns again to establish the new heavens and the new earth. When that happens, Mr. and Mrs. *Eikon* will bask in the glory of union with God, where they will themselves be so radiant as to draw attention to God's oneness as the origin of it all.

This, or something quite close, is the plot of the story that Jesus expects everyone to use to tell their wiki-stories. I am tempted as a Bible teacher to work this out now for every book in the Bible, for each wiki-story of the Story. But this book is not an introduction to the Bible. Instead, it is about how we are to live the Bible out and how blue parakeets force us to rethink how we read the Bible. This means that we need an example, and I have chosen how women are gifted to perform ministries in the church as our example. This issue will reveal how reading the Bible as a oneness-otherness-oneness story gives us discernment for today. But before we get to that discussion, we want to delve into an element of Bible reading that is nearly always neglected:

If the Bible is Story, how do we read it?
The answer: We listen to God.
Thus the question means: What is our relationship to the Bible?

Turn the page.

Part 2

Listening

What Do I Do with the Bible?

Therefore everyone who hears these words of mine and puts them into practice is like a wise man who built his house on the rock. The rain came down, the streams rose, and the winds blew and beat against that house; yet it did not fall, because it had its foundation on the rock. But everyone who hears these words of mine and does not put them into practice is like a foolish man who built his house on sand. The rain came down, the streams rose, and the winds blew and beat against that house, and it fell with a great crash.

Jesus, according to Matthew 7:24 – 27

Chapter 6

From Paper to Person

How Do We Read God's Words?

A student of mine majoring in art brought a piece of her artwork to class. Before others had found the way to their seats, she brought it to me, placed it in front of me, and with a little flush in her face said, "I thought you might like to see this."

Well, of course, I did, and because the artist was standing next to me and because I wanted to be sensitive to her personal creation, I took a good, long look at it and said, "I really like this." Then I asked her the common question art students don't want to answer: "What are you trying to say in this?"

Again, a little more flush in the face, and her response: "What do you see?" Two things were going on here. First, she cared deeply what I saw in that piece and wasn't about to tell me what she was trying to say. Second and even more important, this piece of art was deeply personal to her. It said something from the depth of her soul. It was a revelation of her heart. She put her soul on display in her piece of work in order to evoke response from others.

The Bible is like this. It is the creation of God, who is the Artist, and the Artist stands next to us as we read the Bible. I sometimes think we forget what we are reading. The Bible is *God's* story. When I say this, I am making a claim so extraordinary we may be tempted to skip over it. The Bible, so we believe, is unlike all other books because these words are *God's* words, this book is *God's* book, and this story is *God's* story.

Knowing that the Bible is God's story and that God stands next to us as we read it leads to an important question: How do we read a story that we claim is *God's* story? To dig deeper than these questions, we need to ask a better one: "What is my *relationship* to the Bible?" This question is one of the most important questions we can ask about reading the Bible, and I am a little startled that so many who talk about the Bible skip over the question. Too many stop short by asking only, "How can I learn to understand the Bible?"

Now let me continue by saying that even that question is not good enough. The real question at the bottom of all of them is this: "What is my relationship to the *God* of the Bible?" Our relationship is not so much with the Bible but with the *God* of the Bible. There's a difference that makes a big difference.

Deep Inside

I grew up with a specific kind of approach to the Bible, and it has taken me a long time to develop a more complete understanding of the Bible. I grew up with what might be called the "authority approach" to the Bible. Simply put, it works with these words: God, revelation, inspiration, inerrancy, authority, and submission. Let me summarize: God *revealed* himself in the Bible. To make sure the Bible's authors got things right, God's Spirit was at work *inspiring* what they wrote. Because God, who is always true, produced the Bible, it is *inerrant* (without error). As God's true Word, therefore, it is our final *authority*, and our response to the Bible must be one of *submission*. I believe this is an approach that fosters a relationship with the Bible.

Deep inside I knew there was something wrong with framing our view of the Bible like this. It took me years to put my finger on it. Perhaps I can say it like this: When I read my Bible, the words "authority" and "submission" don't describe the dynamic I experience. It is not that I think these words are wrong, but I know there is far more to reading the Bible than submitting to authority.

As a college student one of my favorite chapters of the Bible was Psalm 119. Why? Because the psalmist and I shared something: we both loved God's Word, and we both loved to study its words. But the psalmist's approach to his Bible—and you can just sit down and read it—is not expressed like this: "Your words are authoritative, and I am called to submit to them." Instead, his approach is more like this: "Your words are delightful, and I love to do what you ask." The difference between these two approaches is enormous. One of them is a relationship to the Bible; the other is a relationship with God.

Here are some of my favorite lines from Psalm 119, and it is out of words like these that a "relational approach" to the Bible can be formed:

I delight in your decrees; I will not neglect your word (v. 16).
My soul is consumed with longing for your laws at all times (v. 20).
Your statutes are my delight; they are my counselors (v. 24).
Direct me in the path of your commands, for there I find delight
    (v. 35).
I will walk about in freedom, for I have sought out your precepts
    (v. 45).
For I delight in your commands because I love them (v. 47).
Your decrees are the theme of my song wherever I lodge (v. 54).
You are good, and what you do is good; teach me your decrees (v. 68).
The law from your mouth is more precious to me than thousands of
    pieces of silver and gold (v. 72).
How sweet are your words to my taste, sweeter than honey to my
    mouth! (v. 103).
Your statutes are wonderful; therefore I obey them (v. 129).

Here is perhaps the entire psalm in one line: "I have sought your face with all my heart" (v. 58). God's face! How cool is that? A relational approach to the Bible finds room for words like "delight" and "my soul is consumed" and "counselors" and "freedom" and "love" and the "theme of my song" and "good" and "precious" and "sweet" and "wonderful." The view of Scripture I grew up with didn't have room for such words. Deep inside I knew there was more.

What I learned about the authority approach to the Bible was that it is not personal enough or relational enough. It does not express enough of why it is that God gave us the Bible.

What Do You Teach?

I'm a professor, and every November, Bible and religion professors gather together for an academic conference. Truth be told, the best thing about this conference is that we get to see our academic friends. Gathering with friends introduces us to our friends' friends. Such casual conversation leads to a common question: "What do you teach?" I've been asked this question hundreds of times. We wear name tags, but no one's name tag says (as is the case with a friend of mine), "Professor Ben Witherington III" and then under that the subject matter: "New Testament." Rather, our name tags have our name and the school we teach at. So, Ben's says, "Asbury Theological Seminary." We can only guess what each professor teaches.

One time, as a young professor, I asked the common professorial question to a wise and gentle professor: "What do you teach?" His response stunned me: "I teach students. What do you teach?" He made me realize in a new way what I am actually called to do. I wager that about 99 percent of professors who have been asked that question will give you the subject matter they teach — Old Testament, New Testament, Judaism, church history, systematic theology, and the like. That wise professor's answer and question changed how I approach what I do. I need to remind myself of this as I enter the class: I'm not teaching just a subject matter (Jesus' temptations) but *students* who need to come into contact with the subject matter.

The standard approach, where the focus is teaching a subject, is not relational and personal enough. Teachers are teaching *students* a particular subject matter. They are not teaching a subject matter to students. The difference is a big difference.

So, what I'm saying is that the authority approach to the Bible is not enough. There is more to the Bible than its subject matter. In fact, the dynamic involved is earth-shattering and ought to revolutionize how we approach the Bible. It is, as noted above, the *relational approach*. So, let me build a relational approach to the Bible, one that finds resonance with the delightful obedience of the psalmist, one that sees God's words as personal words, and let me see what you think. I will focus on five ideas that will fill out what we mean by reading the Bible as Story so we can learn to live it out. The relational approach turns the Bible from facts-only to facts-that-lead-to-engagement with the God of the Bible.

The Relational Approach to the Bible

God and the Bible

The relational approach *distinguishes God from the Bible*. God existed before the Bible existed; God exists independently of the Bible now. God is a person; the Bible is paper. God gave us this papered Bible to lead us to love his person. But the person and the paper are not the same.

The distinction between a person's words and the person is an important one, but I am not sure we Christians have always made that distinction. Perhaps this will make it clear: I love my wife, Kris; I do not love Kris's words. I encounter Kris through her words, but I am summoned to love her, not her words. Sometimes I say to her, "I love what you say to me," but that is a form of expression. What I'm really saying is, "I love you, and your words communicate that love to me."

We need to see the same distinction with the Bible. If we don't, we set ourselves up for problems. Even when the psalmist says he loves God's commands, the larger context shows that it is God whom he loves, and God's words extend the person onto paper. Notice how often the psalmist says "you" in Psalm 119; my TNIV has forty-two such occurrences, as in "You are my portion, LORD" (Psalm 119:57). Notice also how often he says "I" (109 times). This combination of "you" and "I" is a revelation of the relational approach. A relational approach seeks a relationship with the person behind the paper words "I" and "you" in Psalm 119.

Missing the difference between God and the Bible is a bit like the person who reads Jonah and spends hours and hours figuring out if a human can live inside a whale—and what kind of whale it was—but never encounters God. The book is about Jonah's God, not Jonah's whale. Or it is like the athlete who becomes enamored with her soccer uniform and forgets that she's got a game to play regardless of what the uniform looks like. Or perhaps it is like a college student who, like, forgets that the point of college is, like, studying and learning and not (only) finding a wonderful social life. Or it is like the person who is obsessed with the appearance of the church building and misses that the point of the building is facilitation of worship and fellowship, of loving God and loving others.

True, you can't have Jonah's prophecy without the whale, you can't have a soccer game without some uniforms, you can't have college without social relations, and it is harder to conduct a worship service without some sacred space; but the first element is distinguishable from the second. So it is with God and the Bible. Once again, God speaks to us in words but God is more than the Bible.

Here, then, is our first step in a proper relationship with the Bible: we must distinguish God from the Bible.

God ≠ Bible

Bible as God's Written Communication

A relational approach also focuses on the Bible as *God's written communication with us*. The Bible is like a spoken message or a letter from

God addressed to God's people, not unlike the words we might speak or write in order to communicate something to someone we love. Once again, we must pause briefly to consider what we are saying. God is not the Bible. To make the Bible into God is idolatrous.

The Bible is God's communication — in the form of words — with us. We can trot out here all the important words about the Bible — inspiration, revelation, truth, etc. — and they deserve to be. But those are not enough. Behind all of these words is the astounding claim we Christians make: the Bible is God's communication with us in the form of words. For the papered book to be what it is intended to be, God's communication with us, we need to receive those words as God's words addressed to God's people.

God communicates → Bible → with God's people

Listening

If we are invited to love God by reading the Bible as God's communication with us, then a relational approach to the Bible invites us *to listen to God (the person) speak in the Bible and to engage God as we listen.* The relational approach knows the Bible is filled with wiki-stories — timely stories of the Story by human authors. But our approach believes the Bible is more than human wiki-stories. These authors are *divinely guided so that their wiki-stories tell God's story.* If we once admit this, we are summoned to stand in front of the Bible as *those listening to God's story.* (We may argue with God and the Bible and we may ask questions, but that all comes after we listen; our next chapter will explore the theme of listening.)

God communicates → Bible → with God's *listening* people

Bible and the Big Conversation

One of my favorite discoveries about the relational approach is that we enter into *the Bible's own conversation and the conversation the church has had about the Bible.* The Bible is a lively conversation of one author or prophet or apostle with one another as each listens to God speaking. If you read Deuteronomy and then read Job—I know, that is not a typical evening's reading—you observe that Job is engaging Deuteronomy in a serious conversation. Yes, Job says to Moses, there is a correlation between obedience and blessing, but there is more to it than that. Job learned, and God reveals to us, that sometimes God is at work outside the correlation of obedience and blessing.

Another example: Most of us, after reading James say that we are justified not by faith alone but by works (James 2:24), recognize that James is in conversation with Paul, with someone like Paul, or with someone who is distorting Paul. Paul emphasizes justification by faith and James emphasizes works, and reading these two in the web of an ongoing conversation puts each in his proper context.

And there's a second conversation going on. Just as the biblical authors converse with one another, so Christians in the history of the church have conversed with one another—about the Bible's own conversation. Some, as we sketched in the second chapter, believe we can ignore what God has said to others; they leapfrog over the history of the church to return to the Bible all alone. This approach, sadly, ignores the conversation God has directed throughout the history of the church. But if we learn to read the Bible *with* tradition—and it's a bit like sitting down at table with three or four generations in our family on Christmas holiday—we can enter into this big conversation in which we can learn from the wisdom of the past. Our privilege and our challenge is to carry on that conversation in our world today.

God communicates → Bible → God's listening people
in conversation

Relationship with God

I bring it all together into one central focus now: A relational approach believes *our relationship to the Bible is transformed into a relationship with the God who speaks to us in and through the Bible.* We come back now to our first observation: If we distinguish God from the Bible, then we also learn that in listening to God's words in the Bible we are in search of more than a relationship with paper with words, namely, a relationship with the person who speaks on paper. *Our relationship to the Bible is actually a relationship with the God of the Bible.* We want to emphasize that we don't ask what the Bible says, we ask what God says to us in that Bible. The difference is a difference between paper and person.

God communicates → Bible → God's listening people
in conversation
↓
relationship with God of the Bible

Let me put this now one final way: God gave the Bible not so we can know *it* but so we can know and love God through *it*.

Professors and Their Administrators

Maybe another analogy will point us in the right direction. My relationship to the president and provost and dean of my university, North Park University, might be called a relationship of authority. David Parkyn, our president, Joseph Jones, our provost, and Charles Peterson, our dean, are in one sense authority figures. They have more authority than I do—and they should have. Frankly, knowing the kind of life an administrator is called to live, I am quite happy to cede that authority to them. Actually, I'm not ceding anything to them. They are given authority by the board of trustees, and my responsibility is to acknowledge their authority. However you look at it, they have a kind of authority I don't.

However, it's all about framing the relationship. If I frame their relationship to me in terms of authority—as in "They are my authority figures"—then I have to frame my relationship to them in terms of submission—as in "I do whatever they say." If a professor's responsibility is simply one of submission—which it isn't at our school, since these authority figures engage each of us at the level of personal and professional conversations that sometimes lead to disagreement—the whole relationship is framed by words like "hierarchy," "authority," and "obedience."

Is this a proper way of framing the relationship of an administrator and a professor? I hope not. In fact, if an administrator chooses to frame his or her relationship to professors in terms of authority—as in "I am in charge. Listen to me. Do this or that!"—then the dynamic heart of the relationship has gone south. Administrators who appeal to this are usually in trouble. If a man or woman frames his or her relationship to a spouse or to children in terms of the word "authority," you can bet your sweet bippy that the relationship is not what it should be.

What if we frame our relationship differently? What if, instead of framing a professor's relationship to the administration in terms of authority, we frame it in terms of love, trust, and conversation? To be sure, within that frame there is authority and sometimes debate and disagreement. I've had my share of that. But the point we are making is that the framing of the relationship is very important. What words do we use that best frame such a relationship? I am certain of this, authority and submission are not the best terms.

Let's extend this to another realm. For reasons better left untouched right now, traditional Christians have framed the relationship of a husband and a wife in terms of hierarchy, authority, and submission. Why? Because Paul and Peter use such terms in their letters (see Ephesians 5:21–33 and 1 Peter 3:1–7). Apart from studying these passages more carefully in their own contexts, which a story reading of the Bible insists on, when we frame a husband-wife relationship in such terms, we are surely making a serious mistake. There's a lot more to it than this. Any relationship of a husband and wife that is not foremost a frame of love will distort the relationship.

The story of the Bible has one book devoted to husbands and wives, the Song of Songs, and before one ever reads Ephesians 5 or 1 Peter 3, one should dip deeply into the Song's intimate secrets. The framing of a husband and wife relationship in terms of love—the kind of delightful, playful love found in the Song of Songs—completely changes things.

So, too, if we frame our relationship to the Bible in terms of authority, we will inevitably have authoritarian issues emerging as theology. Here is a conclusion that has taken me nearly thirty years to come to: without denying the legitimacy of the various terms in the authority approach, those who have a proper relationship to the Bible *never need to speak of the Bible as their authority nor do they speak of their submission to the Bible.* They are so in tune with God, so in love with him, that the word "authority" is swallowed up in loving God. Even more, the word "submission" is engulfed in the disposition of listening to God speak through the Bible and in the practice of doing what God calls us to do.

Once we come to terms with the relational approach of the Bible and we frame the Bible as God's story in the form of a plot with wiki-stories, we begin to think about our *relationship to the Bible.* If submission falls short of how we respond to the Bible, what word best captures our response to the Bible? Turn the page.

Chapter 7

God Speaks, We Listen

What Is Our Relationship to the God Who Speaks to Us in the Bible?

A student sat in my office one day when he turned our conversation to the right set of beliefs about the Bible. His observation: "Why does my youth pastor ask me all the time if I still believe in the 'inerrancy' of the Bible?" I was about to explain to him the history of the doctrine of Scripture and the battles Christians have waged over the Bible when he interrupted me with these words (and this is how he said it): "You know, Scot, I really don't give a d—n what my youth pastor's view of the Bible is because he doesn't give one frickin' dime to the poor and he's never met a homeless person in his life and he didn't even know about Darfur when I mentioned it to him at Christmas." This student was obviously now a bit worked up, so I sat back to listen.

He continued: "My view of the Bible is this: I read it often — not every day — and I *do* what I think God tells me to do. I don't make much money, but I give" — he was about to tell me what percent he gave to the poor but stopped himself because he thought it might be self-congratulatory. Then he asked a pointed question, a good one: "What good is 'inerrancy' if you don't *do* what God says?" Then he asked a question that shook me a bit: "If I do what God says, doesn't that show that my view of the Bible is the right one?" Students, you gotta love 'em.

How many of us know our *doctrine* about the Bible but don't *do what the God of the Bible says*? To paraphrase our Lord's brother, "What good is it, my brothers and sisters, if people claim to have the [right view of the Bible] but do not practice what it says?" (James 2:14, retooled). Believing in inspiration, revelation, infallibility or inerrancy, and authority describes one's *view* of the Bible. Fine. We need to talk about our view of the Bible. But that isn't enough.

We have too many today who say, "Now that you've got the right view of the Bible, you're on the side of the angels." Having the right view isn't the point of the Bible. We need to have not only a "view" of the Bible but also a "relationship" to the God of the Bible. *Knowing* water will hydrate the body and *believing* that drinking five bottles of water daily is healthy are not the same as *drinking* the water until one's body is properly hydrated. Those who drink the water are the ones who really know and really believe. Having the right view of the Bible is knowing and believing, but we need to move to the next step: engaging the God of that Bible.

Jesus told a parable that perfectly teaches this point. It is called the parable of the two sons (see Matthew 21:28–32); I give the parable part:

> "What do you think? There was a man who had two sons. He went to the first and said, 'Son, go and work today in the vineyard.'
>
> "'I will not,' he answered, but later he changed his mind and went.
>
> "Then the father went to the other son and said the same thing. He answered, 'I will, sir,' but he did not go.
>
> "Which of the two did what his father wanted?"
>
> "The first," they answered.

Agreeing-and-not-doing and not-agreeing-but-finally-doing are two different things. A relational approach focuses on the second.

We must begin an entirely new conversation that gets us beyond the right *view* of the Bible to one that seeks to answer this question: "What is our *relationship* to the God of the Bible?" I suggest that the answer to that question, and one that comes to mind immediately for the one who reads the Bible attentively, is simple: Our relationship to the God of the Bible is *to listen to God so we can love him more deeply and love others more completely.* If God's ultimate design for us is to love God and to love others, we can only acquire that love by learning to listen to God.

Listening and loving are intimately connected.

Yo, Scot, You Doin' Anything?

A student knocked on my door one fall during the first week of classes. "Yo, Scot, you doin' anything?" she asked.

"No, of course not," I said in what has to be one of my more common understatements. "Come on in." You should know that the average college student spends nine hours a week studying. If that same student were taking sixteen hours of credit, that means she would be occupied with being a student twenty-five hours a week. You do the math.

She sat down in a chair next to me and asked me without a moment's hesitation, "What do you think about homosexuality?" To which I thought to myself, *Wow, that's a big question to ask a teacher you've seen exactly once.* She must have realized that, so she quickly asked another, "What do you think of the war in Iraq?"

Now I had a flashing insight. I knew this student wasn't in my office to ask questions or to look for answers to big questions. She wanted to talk to one of her professors. Having had experience at this, I sensed she was homesick and wanted to be with a parent-like figure. So I asked her about herself, and she asked me a brief question about my blog and my wife and my kids. I then asked her a question, and for the next twenty minutes she went on in a nonstop prattle. Suddenly looking at her cell phone, which doubles as a watch, she exclaimed, "Ohmigosh [that's one word nowadays]! I'm late for class." She slung her backpack over her shoulder, hurried out the door, down the steps, and then, as if realizing she hadn't quite made closure, yelled back, "This was fun. Let's do it again sometime!" *Sure*, I thought.

This student grew to see me as one of her favorite professors for one reason: I had enough time to listen to her. I never quite knew what she saw in me, but I was all ears for her on many occasions. She would stop by—"Yo, Scot, you doin' anything?" (No, of course not.)—and we would chat and I would listen and then she would leave. Sometimes that's all it takes. Listening and loving, we must never forget, are connected.

Kris and I talk all the time; she asks me about my day and I talk my way through the day. I ask her about her day, and she talks her way through her day. Then we're done. I don't think we say to ourselves, "Now, I'm listening; listening is loving; therefore, I'm loving now." Instead, listening to one another is our mode of existence. (I must confess that I'm nowhere near the listener Kris is.)

Reading the Bible is an act of listening. Listening, to quote the title of a popular book, is an act of love.[1]

Listening as Love of God and Others

The most perceptive book about how to listen to the Bible is by Alan Jacobs, a professor at Wheaton College. Jacobs reminds us that *words matter because words flow out of persons*. In *A Theology of Reading: The Hermeneutics of Love*, Jacobs articulates a theory of reading that emerges from two important observations:

1. Written words are *personal* communication from one person to another.
2. The proper relationship of a Christian to a person's communication is to *love* that person by *listening* to their words.[2]

Words on a page, Jacobs informs us over and over, are not just little squiggles of information on paper. Written words are personal exchanges, personal deposits of a person. Our words come from the depth of our heart and soul, and they extend who we are. That is why we care what others think of what we say. Not everything we say is this serious, of course. When I say "How much?" at the grocery store, not too much is on the line (unless, of course, I don't have enough money in my pocket). But statements like "I love you," and questions like "Will you be here for me?" and promises like "I will be with you" are personal exchanges. Words matter because they represent persons. *Because words represent persons, how we respond to words matters.*

When someone writes me an email, it is far easier for me to disagree with the words, scan what has been said, or even casually dismiss the words than if the person were standing in front of me and saying the same thing. I am much more likely, and you probably are too, to listen to a person than to an email. In fact, it would be unchristian to refuse to listen to, to ignore, or to dismiss a person facing me. Jacobs reminds us that the Christian summons to love our neighbor as ourselves, what I call the "Jesus Creed," teaches us that *written words are as serious as the spoken word.*

Jacobs call this Christian understanding of words "the hermeneutics of love." "The hermeneutics of love requires that books and authors ... be understood and treated as neighbors."[3] This means that when our neighbors speak, we listen. Love listens.

Listening in the Bible

Did you know that the word "listen" or "hear" is found more than 1,500 times in the Bible? Klyne Snodgrass, a friend and colleague, studied each of these references and came to this realization: "The biggest complaint in Scripture is that people do not listen to God. Theirs is a freely chosen deafness." Choosing not to listen contradicts the *Shema*: "Hear, O Israel ... Love the LORD your God" (Deuteronomy 6:4–5). Klyne then reached this insightful conclusion: "The greatest command is to love God; the prior command [to loving God] is the command to hear."[4] Love of God and love of others can happen only when we have ears to listen to God speak.

The word "hear" or "listen" in the Bible operates on at least three levels (I will provide my own translations): attention, absorption, and action. *Attention* opens our ears. If you've ever been around a group of people speaking a language you don't know, you instantly recognize what Paul meant in 1 Corinthians 14:2: "For those who speak in a [spiritual] tongue do not speak to other people but to God. Humans do not *attend to* what they are saying [because they cannot understand it]; they are speaking mysteries by the Spirit." (pers. translation)

A second, deeper level of meaning can be found in Solomon's great prayer request after he became king. This expression pertains to *absorption*, when our ears let God's voice in so that it fills our being: "So give your servant a [*hearing*] heart" (1 Kings 3:9). And God did give him a "wise and discerning heart" (3:12), a heart that fully absorbed what God was saying.

The third level puts legs on the ears as *action*, as Jesus says: "Therefore everyone who *hears* these words of mine and puts them into practice" (Matthew 7:24). Or when the Father says to the disciples of Jesus when he was transfigured: "*Listen* to him!" (17:5, emphasis added in both passages). Both of these uses speak of a listening that has ears that lead to certain behaviors.

When we read the Bible as Story and develop a relationship with the God of the Bible,

- we learn to *listen* to and for God in the Bible as we read it;
- we are *attentive* enough to recognize God's voice and let it in;
- we *absorb* what God says so that it floods our inner being; and
- we *act* on what we have heard from God.

Listening to our fellow humans is an art, and you need to get better at listening. So do I. Listening to the Bible is also an art, and you need to get better at that as well. So do I. Sometimes we don't listen. Another way of saying this is that sometimes we listen but not well — there is some attention, but no absorption and action.

Not Listening

I was fifteen. My driver's education instructor had directed me to Reed Park in Freeport, Illinois. This park was near the Little League diamond, where there was a parking lot made of a series of graveled ovals around which and through which we beginners all learned to turn a vehicle safely and accurately. On this day it was my turn to learn how to drive backward, which I was about to learn was no piece of cake.

At the western end of the parking lot my instructor directed me to stop the car and begin backing up. I listened (in the sense of attended) to him and began to do what I thought he had instructed me to do. Next to the lot and to my left was a slight hill, maybe three feet high, extending the length of the lot. Somehow I managed to get the wheels out of line and the car ended up with the driver's side on that hill and the instructor's side still on the gravel oval. Our pitch was not yet dangerous but we were both leaning left to maintain our balance.

He gave me some instruction, to which I listened (in the sense of attended to), but whatever it was, it got reversed in my brain (because I did not absorb what he was saying). The situation got worse as I continued to back even farther up the hill, and my actions showed it. I really was stuck and frustrated as only a fifteen-year-old male (now thoroughly shamed in public) can be.

I stopped the car, put it in park, and offered a suggestion that indicated I was not listening to his instruction — in the sense of attention, absorption, and action! My suggestion to my teacher: that I drive forward out of this mess and start all over. My teacher was convinced I wouldn't learn from this mistake, so he refused to let me drive forward out of the mess. I "listened" — to use a word that is no longer making sense to what was really going on — to his advice again, put the car in reverse, and began moving backward and the situation got a little worse. Now both of us were on the hill, and I was frustrated and said it was impossible to back out of this situation. I quickly put the car in forward and began to drive forward when my instructor slammed down his brake and said, "Put it in reverse!" I had stopped listening and was now talking and seeing everything my way. (You might say I was a Rorschach driver looking for some blessings and promises, and I was getting the law book thrown at me by the maestro to my right, who had the puzzle all put together.)

With the car stopped, I got into a bit of an argument and frustration heated up into stronger words. I demanded that I drive forward to get out of the mess, and he said, "Listen to what I say and you will get out of this mess."

I said to him, with the car now in reverse and now both of us in a coordinated set of leans, "No way, it's impossible."

With his foot on the brake and my frustration now beyond my capacity, I did a fifteen-year-old thing. I put the car in park, pushed open the door, pulled myself out of the car, shut the door, and began to walk home. I had had enough. As I got around the corner and up the street about a half a block, my teacher drove by, gave the car a little honk, and waved at me. He must have been saying to himself, "Yo, Scot, doin' anything?" I nodded my head, thinking that I had at least escaped the shame, and kept walking.

Did I mention the driver's education teacher was my father?

About two weeks later my father suggested we continue the driver's education lessons. He didn't have to mention that our next lesson would be on learning how to drive in reverse. I was more ready to listen, and I think I absorbed and acted on his words. (I never back up without thinking of that event in Reed Park.)

David, a Nonlistener

The Bible is filled with people who, by *not* listening to God, became saintly folks acting sinfully. Take David as an example. David knew what Moses said in Deuteronomy 17:17: the king "must not take many wives, or his heart will be led astray. He must not accumulate large amounts of silver and gold." David heard this (attentiveness), but he didn't listen (absorption, action). Instead, David accumulated wives and concubines:

> Michal, daughter of Saul
> Abigail, widow of Nabal of Carmel
> Ahinoam of Jezreel
> Maacah, daughter of Talmai king of Geshur
> Haggith
> Abital
> Egdah
> A bundle of others according to 2 Samuel 3:13–16
> Ten concubines according to 2 Samuel 15:16
> Bathsheba intentionally widowed from Uriah the Hittite
>   (2 Samuel 11–12)
> Abishag (1 Kings 1–2)

A colossal example of not listening. His son, Solomon, had 700 princess wives and 300 concubines (1 Kings 11:3). He must have been on steroids!

Love Listens

But thankfully, the Bible is also filled with examples of goodly and godly folks who paid attention, absorbed, and then acted on the words of God. Abraham, Joseph, and Josiah are the first ones who come to mind for me. You may think of others. It's all about listening, the kind of listening that leads us to love God and to love others. The apostle Paul did not put the word "listen" in his list of what love is like in 1 Corinthians 13, but he would agree with any of us who join Alan Jacobs by saying, "Love listens."

Alan Jacobs' fine study, mentioned above, leads me to this question: "What would Bible reading look like if it were to be governed by 'the love chapter'?" I read Paul's words in 1 Corinthians 13:4–7 and see in these words a blueprint for reading the Bible. If love listens, then listening to God in the Bible will look like Paul's virtues of love. Add the word "listening" to each of these lines and see what happens:

> Listening love is patient;
> listening love is kind;
> listening love is not envious or boastful or arrogant or rude.
> It does not insist on its own way;
> it is not irritable or resentful;
> it does not rejoice in wrongdoing, but rejoices in the truth.
> It bears all things,
> believes all things,
> hopes all things,
> endures all things.

Good reading is an act of love and therefore an act of listening. But good listening, good attentive listening, good loving listening, is more than gathering information. It is more than just sitting around the back porch with God as we sip tea while God tells us his story. God speaks to us for a reason—I call this "missional" listening. In brief, God tells his story so we can enter into a relationship with him, listen to him, and live out his Word in our day and in our way.

Chapter 8

The Boring Chapter
(on Missional Listening)

What Does God Want to Happen
to Listeners?

After reading the present chapter, Kris referred to it as "the boring chapter" and kept asking me if I had made it better. It was not that she thought it had bad ideas, but she thought it was too theoretical and more than once asked me if I really needed this chapter. I can say I have hacked away and reshaped this chapter a number of times, and I know one thing: it's not as boring as it once was. If you get bored, skip to the next chapter. But let me begin with a story; maybe that will help.

A few years back I taught a course at North Park called "Methods in Bible Study." I believe it is important to read the Bible *with* tradition, so one of our textbooks was by the great fourth-century church father St. Augustine, called *On Christian Doctrine*.[1] Augustine's book was the ancient church's equivalent of our *How to Read the Bible for All It's Worth*.[2] What I read in Augustine's book annoyed me and delighted me at the same time. It gave a method that undid everything I was teaching my students and yet told them everything I ultimately wanted to say. Why? Because it made the bold claim that if the Bible leads the reader to be more loving, then the Bible has accomplished its mission. What annoyed me was that the mission was accomplished whether or not we have interpreted the passage with historical precision and contextual accuracy.

Of course, someone would have immediately called good ole Augustine on the spot for suggesting accurate interpretation doesn't matter. Augustine anticipated that, so he offered a graphic image. Getting the right result of becoming more loving, even if we aren't as accurate in our interpretation as he'd prefer, is like a person on a journey who gets lost but somehow finds the way to the right destination.[3] It is not as if Augustine thought every interpretation was as good as any other. Augustine wrote shelves of commentaries on books of the Bible; he knew how to turn his finger into a pointer and his quill into a torch when he thought he had to. But Augustine knew the Bible's main mission: so that we can become people who love God and love others. If our reading of the Bible leads to this, the mission is accomplished. If it isn't ...

Here is a sad fact: many of those who teach us how to read the Bible teach us how to gather information and find the right path from A to B. They teach us about words and paragraphs and book outlines, and they point us to sources and resources for understanding the historical context. Each of these is important. But what Bible study books don't focus on is church and personal transformation. Any method of Bible study that doesn't lead to transformation abandons the missional path of God and leaves us stranded.

So what is God's missional focus in giving us the story of the Bible? In one expression, it is to give us facts so that we will move those facts into relationship, character, and action.

The Relational Approach Is Missional

The relational approach to the Bible goes beyond normal methods to take us to the heart of what reading the Bible is all about. What is that heart? I can think of no better place than Paul's words to Timothy in 2 Timothy 3:14 – 17. This and Psalm 119 are the most significant passages in the Bible when it comes to the Bible talking about itself. It tells us that God gave the Bible a mission: God speaks to us so we will be the kind of people he wants and will live the way he wants us to live. Read the verses below quietly until you get to the beginning of verse 17, and then forcefully announce (unless you are in a public place) the first two words of verse 17:

> But as for you, continue in what you have learned and have become convinced of, because you know those from whom you learned it, and how from infancy you have known the Holy Scriptures, which are able to make you wise for salvation through faith in Christ Jesus. All Scripture is God-breathed and is useful for teaching, rebuking, correcting and training in righteousness, [17]SO THAT all God's people may be thoroughly equipped for every good work.

Everything leads to verse 17, where we come face-to-face with a big fat "so that." Educators know that teaching *begins at the end, with outcomes*, with the "so thats" of education. Outcome-based education means we ask this question as we prepare and teach: "What do we want our students *to be* and to be able *to do* at the end of this course, this major, and this degree?" We no longer ask just what we want students *to know*—measured normally by exams and papers—but we want to know what students are able *to do with what they know*. In our department at North Park University, we have three major outcomes, three major "so thats":

- knowledge of Bible, theology, and church history
- critical thinking skills
- responsibility of knowledge for shaping identity and behavior

That is, we want our students to know some facts, we want them to be able to think about faith reasonably, and we want them to practice what they believe. We cannot promise they will achieve each of these, but we shape our courses toward these "so that" outcomes. By the way, the word "outcome" for me is gobbledygook English from a group of people I call "educrats," whose job it is to run from school to school to make sure professors are accomplishing something measurable. The word "outcome" makes me think of what our plumber pulls out of our sewer. But "educrats," most of whom must not have done well in English classes, have worked themselves into a position to decide which terms teachers must use. We now use this word as often as our students use the word "like," as in "she was, like, so late to class," and as often as our politicians use the word "balance," as in "balance the budget."

God, too, is interested in "outcomes," though I'm not sure he'd approve of the word, so the Bible uses "so that." To get to the outcomes we have to go through a sequence of thoughts for Paul, unmasking the four stages for missional listening as he writes to Timothy—but remember that everything is aimed at that "so that." Everything! Any reading of any passage in the Bible, the whole Story, that doesn't end up with the "so that" of 2 Timothy 3:17 is not done.

Missional Listening

Missional Listening Begins with the Wisdom of the Ages

Paul begins where we left off in an earlier chapter: he exhorts Timothy to read the Bible *with* the tradition, not *through* the tradition, and certainly not all by himself. Timothy has been formed by those who knew the gospel. Here's what Paul says to him in 2 Timothy 3:14–15.

> But as for you, continue in what you have learned and have become convinced of, *because you know those from whom you learned it*, and how from infancy you have known the Holy Scriptures, which are able to make you wise for salvation through faith in Christ Jesus. (emphasis added)

As Phil Towner, who has written the finest commentary we have today on this letter of Paul, deftly observes, "The teaching is only as good as its teachers."[4] I would add "the teaching is also *just* as good as its teachers."

Judaism is known for its mastery of Torah and Talmud. It is also known for teachers who not only *know* but *observe*. Such was the world in which Jesus and Paul lived. When we think of teaching in the first century, we dare not let ourselves think of a classroom with desks and inkpots and papyrus scrolls bundled up on a library shelf at the back of the room. Or of a teacher in the front of a room lecturing away as students were doing what they could to stay awake and memorize their lessons so they would pass the next test. Nor should we think of learning as simply amassing information. Instead, we need to think of a Jesus and a Paul who were out and about engaging folks in conversation, with disciples hanging around them, asking questions, and studiously watching the behaviors of Jesus and Paul. In other words, education for them was not simply information; it was also formation. Education was training in righteousness and in good works. It was more like a golf lesson than a classroom lecture.

Timothy's teachers were two women — his mother and grandmother (2 Timothy 1:5; 3:14) — and the apostle Paul (3:10 – 11). Missional listening begins with wise mentors, such as those of Timothy.

Slide and Land

You have no doubt either been to or seen a waterslide in a big theme park. Confession time: I've been to water parks, I've watched my children at water parks, but — here's my excuse — sliding down a slide (or swinging on a swing) is not a thing I do; it easily disrupts something my doctor calls the "inner ear" and "labyrinthian canals," so I get nausated sliding down slides. So, my illustration here comes from watching my kids when they were young.

Waterslides are long and wide and curvy and have wonderfully banked sides. Water runs down the waterslide freely and abundantly to increase the speed of the slider. What we might not observe is that everything about a trip down the slide and into the pool of water at the bottom is determined by the slide itself; even more important for our safety, where we land is shaped by the slide. Without banked, steep sides we would fly off the slide and ... well, we'd get hurt.

Reading the Bible *with* our wise mentors is like sliding down a waterslide. The gospel is the slide; the Bible is one wall, our teachers and our tradition the other wall, and the water is the Holy Spirit. The pool at the bottom of the slide is our world. If we stay on the slide and inside the walls as we slide down, we will land in our own water world. If we knock down the walls of the slide or get too careless, we can tumble out of the safety of that slide and injure ourselves. However, observe this: our life is lived in the pool. So here's my point: God asks us to listen—attention, absorption, and action—to the gospel story and to read the Bible *with* our wise mentors who have gone before us; if we do so, we will land in the pool in our day and in our way.

But we are getting ahead of ourselves. Missional listening begins with the wisdom of the ages, but there is a special dynamic at work in missional listening that has the capacity to change who we are and how we live.

Missional Listening Is Empowered by Inspiration

Scripture is also *God-breathed* or "inspired." Paul didn't have a New Testament, so when he says "Scripture," he probably means the Old Testament and perhaps some gospel traditions about Jesus and some early apostolic writings (1 Timothy 5:18; 2 Peter 3:15–16). What is most important here is the dynamic Paul is pointing at: the presence of the Spirit who takes words on paper and turns them into the living presence of God speaking to us. Here is where the relational approach reminds us that Scripture, as God-breathed, is God the person speaking to us on paper.

What makes missional listening powerful, what leads the reader into a life of righteousness and good works (the outcomes Paul mentions), is the promise that the Spirit who hovered over the author is the same Spirit at work in the reader. Unfortunately, too many of us spend too much time arguing about the meaning of "inspiration" and not enough on the point of it all. The Spirit who guided the author through a history and a community to the moment when he put quill to papyrus is the same Spirit at work when you and I sit down with our Bible.

What gives us the power for the outcomes is the Spirit.

Missional Listening Is a Process

For years Kris would get home from her office as a psychologist and ask me how my day went. She always asked me what I was studying, and sometimes I would bubble up in a flourish of words. Now before I say anything further, I need to insert this thought: I live and breathe and eat and sleep and walk and play and converse with a woman who is unflaggingly committed to what matters and to what is useful. She knows that "theories" can only go so far; she knows that theology is supposed to involve a *process* leading to real life changes.

One day when she asked what I had studied, I told her I had been studying the participle "going" in the Great Commission and informed her that after hours of study, a good translation would be "Go make disciples!" That, I thought (and still do think), is better than "By going, make disciples" or "Go and make disciples." I had discovered something. Not earth-shattering, of course, but my hard work paid off. Kris thought my translation was clever and, for all she knew, accurate. Then she made another point by asking a question, just the sort of question a psychologist might ask: "So, did you go make any disciples today?" Bingo! The "So what?" question got me. If what I learned wasn't "useful," if the process didn't lead to the "so that" of 2 Timothy 3:17, it wasn't much good. Kris's questions changed my career interests.

My book *The Jesus Creed: Loving God, Loving Others*, which discusses the significance of loving God and loving others as the heart of spiritual formation, emerged from a string of Kris's "So what?" conversations. The point of the book is to get us to recite the Jesus Creed so often that it digs its way into our very bones. One time I said something out of impatience (my besetting sin) to Kris, and she observed in the far room that what I had said "wasn't very Jesus-Creed-like." Ouch. So, a week or so later, Kris said something to me I didn't like, so I informed her that her comment was not very Jesus-Creed-like. Her defense: "I didn't write the book!"

We've played with this banter for a few years now, but underneath it all is a conviction both of us have that God designs all biblical study to be a "useful" process that leads us to the Bible *in such a way that it creates a person who loves God and loves others.* Anything less fails to achieve why God speaks to us in the Bible. God's got a mission in giving us the Bible, and that mission is "useful."

Paul, too, knew the Bible was designed to be "useful." "All Scripture," he says, "is God-breathed and is *useful* for ..." (2 Timothy 3:16, emphasis added). Missional listeners discover we are in a process of being transformed from what we are into what God wants us to be. Here's the process:

> we become informed;
> we get rebuked;
> we are restored; and
> we become instructed in righteousness.[5]

If we are committed to missional listening to God as we read the Bible, we will learn, we will be rebuked about our failures, we will be restored, and—now to use borrow language from our educrats—we will get "outcomed." What is the outcome of this process? *Righteousness.* To be "righteous" means our minds, our wills, and our behaviors will be conformed to God's will. It means holiness, goodness, love, justice, and good works.

It takes time, but missional listening leads to righteousness.

Missional Listening Blossoms into a Life of Good Works

" ... SO THAT all God's people may be thoroughly equipped for every good work" (2 Timothy 3:17).[6] The divine outcome, the divine "so that," of missional listening to the God of the Bible is *good works.* Any reading and any interpretation that does not lead to good works, both as the practical application and as the behavioral result, aborts what the Bible is designed to produce. I know, "aborts" is a strong word, but we need such a word here. God's "so that" is "good works."

What are good works? Peter urged the Christians in Asia Minor to be benevolent in their cities; Paul exhorted the Roman Christians to love their neighbor as themselves; John urged his readers to walk in the light and to love one another; James reminded followers of Jesus to care for widows and orphans, to feed the hungry, and to clothe the naked. Good works are concrete responses to the needs we see in our neighbors.

I don't think any person reading this book wonders *what* good works are. The question is not what they are but whether we are doing them. This passage in Paul leads me to the following two conclusions—and they stare at each of us:

> If you are doing good works, you are reading the Bible aright.
> If you are not doing good works, you are not reading the Bible aright.

If you are in the first group, keep it up; if you are in the second group, make some changes.

Slide and Land, Part Two

Earlier in this chapter I likened missional listening to sliding down a waterslide at a theme park. The slide is the gospel, the walls of that slide are the Bible and our wise mentors (tradition), and the water is the Holy Spirit. I also said that our joy, our delight, our challenge is to enter the slide, to enter the Bible as Story, and to let it take us where we are supposed to go. When that happens, we become people of good works.

I want to turn now in this book to the landing, to what happens to us if we slide down the waterslide. Where will we land? How do we land? Our landing in the water is a process of discernment of learning how to fly from the story of the Bible into our world. Each of us, in fellowship with our community of faith, is called to enter the slide and follow its faithful contours so we can land in the water of our world.

Part 3

Discerning

How Do I Benefit from the Bible?

Though I am free and belong to no one, I have made myself a slave to everyone, to win as many as possible. To the Jews I became like a Jew, to win the Jews. To those under the law I became like one under the law (though I myself am not under the law), so as to win those under the law. To those not having the law I became like one not having the law (though I am not free from God's law but am under Christ's law), so as to win those not having the law. To the weak I became weak, to win the weak. I have become all things to all people so that by all possible means I might save some. I do all this for the sake of the gospel, that I may share in its blessings.

The apostle Paul, according to 1 Corinthians 9:19–23

For this reason, since the day we heard about you, we have not stopped praying for you. We continually ask God to fill you with the knowledge of his will through all the wisdom and understanding that the Spirit gives, so that you may live a life worthy of the Lord and please him in every way.

The apostle Paul, according to Colossians 1:9–10

Chapter 9

The Year of Living Jesus-ly

What Do We Do
and What Do We Not Do
in the Bible?

So how do we apply the Bible to our lives? How do we live out the story of the Bible today? Do we open up a passage, read it, and live it just as it says? Most of will admit that it's not that easy, at least not all the time.

Let's take a quick look in our Bibles at Leviticus 19. Somehow we know what to "pick" and what to "choose" and what "not to pick" and what "not to choose" when we read this chapter. (If you do this in a class, which I have done, ask everyone to vote on those they think we should do and those they think we shouldn't do. You might be surprised by the results.) I call this list of blue parakeet commandments from Leviticus 19 ...

The Commands We Mostly Don't Keep

(check boxes you believe we should observe today)

☑ 1. Be holy because I, the LORD your God, am holy (19:2).
☐ 2. You must observe my Sabbaths. I am the LORD your God (19:3).

☐ 3. When you reap the harvest of your land, do not reap to the very edges of your field or gather the gleanings of your harvest. Do not go over your vineyard a second time or pick up the grapes that have fallen. Leave them for the poor and the foreigner. I am the LORD your God (19:9–10).

☐ 4. Do not go about spreading slander among your people (19:16).

☐ 5. Do not plant your field with two kinds of seed. Do not wear clothing woven of two kinds of material (19:19).

☐ 6. Do not eat any meat with the blood still in it (19:26).

☐ 7. Do not cut the hair at the sides of your head or clip off the edges of your beard (19:27).

☐ 8. Do not ... put tattoo marks on yourselves. I am the LORD (19:28).

☐ 9. Stand up in the presence of the aged (19:32).

☐ 10. Keep all my decrees and all my laws and follow them. I am the LORD (19:37).

Other than #1 and #4, most of us don't follow any of these commands literally. Think about this list carefully because it really does make us rethink how we read the Bible.

- We don't keep the Sabbath (Friday night sundown to Saturday night sundown) [Sunday is not the same as Sabbath].
- We don't harvest only some of our crops (if we even harvest).
- We don't worry about planting two kinds of seed (if we plant at all).
- We don't worry about wearing garments made of more than one substance — cotton and polyester blends, for example (if we even pay attention).
- We don't hesitate to eat medium to rare meats (unless vegetarian).
- We don't have moral issues in cutting our earlocks (at least I don't).
- We (most of us that is) don't think tattoos are sinful.
- We don't always (or ever!) stand up when older folks walk into the room.

These ten commands are never part of a discipleship program; yet they are commanded by God in the Bible. Furthermore, it's not like

Moses is just giving a few good suggestions for special students who want to imitate him. In fact, these commandments are propped up with a profoundly theological comment—"I am the LORD your God." And they all start with an even more profound comment: "because I, the LORD your God, am holy." Moses anchors these commands in the holiness of God. Since God's holiness doesn't change, doesn't it make sense to think God's rules for his people don't change either?

The quick answer to this question is that while God's holiness doesn't change, his will for his people does. This, then, leads to one of my favorite questions: How do we know which of those commandments change and which ones don't? How do we choose? Who gets to choose?

Either we are completely wrong in our dismissal of these commands or we have some categories in our Christian minds to help us know what to apply to our lives and what not to. (I think it is the second option.) To make this more complex, in spite of near-universal dismissal of most of these commandments, some Christians disagree on which of the ten to follow and which not to follow, so some have practiced these since the beginning of the church. Still, most of us would wipe most of these commandments off our moral map. Why? Because, and here I give some typical answers:

> they are from a bygone era; or
> they are from the Old Testament; or
> they are from Leviticus; or
> they are from what many call the Holiness Code; or
> they are from ceremonial codes and we follow only the moral codes.

Or some such set of reasons that really say, "That was then, but this is now." Oddly enough, smack-dab in the middle of this chapter is Leviticus 19:18, one of Jesus' and the early church's favorite commands: "Love your neighbor as yourself." Somehow we know, perhaps because Jesus and the early Christians repeated it so often, that this command in this chapter is applicable to us but many of the others aren't. How do we know this?

Essentially, the church has always taught that the *times have changed and we have learned from New Testament patterns of discernment what to do and what not to do.* Often it is easy; sometimes we have to have a discussion but can agree. At other times it gets difficult. So ...

What about Sex before Marriage?

Most of us believe that premarital sexual intercourse is contrary to God's will. The New Testament doesn't say a thing about this. However, we know the prohibition in Exodus 22 and Deuteronomy 22 (vv. 28–29), we believe premarital sexual intercourse is wrong, and we conclude that the laws of the Old Testament prohibiting such are to be applied today. Exodus 22:16–17 comes at this from a specific angle, the angle of the disgruntled father of the seduced virgin:

> If a man seduces a virgin who is not pledged to be married and sleeps with her, he must pay the bride-price, and she shall be his wife. If her father absolutely refuses to give her to him, he must still pay the bride-price for virgins.

The Old Testament teaches that premarital intercourse is wrong (we accept that), and it obligates the couple to marriage (we're not sure about that one). We like the father's choice and some of us wish the woman would get a voice in this text. But, overall, we think this text gets it permanently right. To make this point abundantly clear to students in whom hormones are pounding into one another, I often say that there is no such thing as "premarital" intercourse in the Bible. Intercourse, I show them from this text, *constitutes the sexual union that we call marriage.* Perhaps it is an overcooked way of saying it, but I get my point across.

Every now and then a historically minded student will ask questions like this: "Well, didn't they marry younger? Isn't it harder for us?" What the student is saying is this: "Haven't the times changed?" What they are implying is this: "Is the regulation the same for us?" I think that's a good question.

Listen to this letter from a reader of my blog, Dianne Parsons, who also knows that the times have changed since the times of the Bible and that these changes, she is suggesting, have enormous implications for the sexual temptations of young adults.

> I would like to see someone thoughtfully address the issue [in today's culture] of the gap of many years between the age of sexual maturity and age at which people enter into marriage. Assuming sexual maturity between age 10 and 15 (and often earlier) and marriage between 25 and 30, there is anywhere between 10 and 20 years of the strongest hormonal influence on sexuality. Yet churches still preach celibacy [she means the traditional view of waiting until marriage] with a straight face to the emerging generation, who mostly turn away.
>
> I see 4 options for those in the emerging generation:
>
> 1) Remain celibate for 1 to 2 decades of the most sexually intense time of their lives;
>
> 2) Marry at a much earlier age than their contemporaries;
>
> 3) Stay away from church [and engage in intercourse] until married and/or with children;
>
> 4) Attend church and compartmentalize that part of their life and keep sexual intercourse "private."
>
> A few choose #1, but let's be honest, most do not. Statistically, it's clear that many do not choose #2, except for those at seminary or Christian colleges. So what about all the others? Do ministry leaders assume that many in the emerging generation can or will be convinced to join group #1? How? By simply preaching "just say no"?

Dianne then asks what I think is a fundamental question for those who want to learn how to "apply" the Bible today are asking:

How can we take a Bible that forbids sex outside of marriage, that was written in a time where there was little or no time that passed between sexual maturity and marriage, and apply it to today's situation? I see this as a significant challenge in ministering to the emerging generation, and I don't see it discussed much.

There it is. Some think of the Bible like this: "God says it, I believe it, that settles it." They treat the Bible the way many treat a trouble-shooting chart at the back of a manual.

> Problem: Premarital sexual temptation.
> Solution: Just say no!
> Response: "That was then, *and* it is *also* now!"

Others, however, are pressing the issue from a different angle. They say something like this as they approach the Bible as a troubleshooting chart:

> Problem: Work on the Sabbath.
> Solution: Keep the Sabbath!
> Response: "That was then, but this is now!"

With a genuine cry of the heart as well as a genuine intellectual question, these same persons get together and ask one another, "Why do we say the rule about premarital sex is to be applied but not the Sabbath one?" They are really asking this question: "Was the prohibition of premarital intercourse shaped exclusively for a culture in which young adults got married at the onset of puberty?"

If you think these are easy questions to answer, I would recommend getting your ear closer to the ground. The issue of "applying" the Bible is not as simple as troubleshooting charts. I think we are learning that there's a lot more *discerning* going on than we thought. It is all about adopting and adapting, and we need to get our leaders together to start thinking about this more.

A Year of Living Biblically

The inspiration for this book has come from years of reading, wondering, living, and teaching the Bible. The inspiration for this next section comes from A. J. Jacobs' funny, insightful, and suggestive (for me) book, *The Year of Living Biblically: One Man's Humble Quest to Follow the Bible as Literally as Possible*.[1] Jacobs grew up in an "extremely secular home" and is "officially Jewish." But, he confesses, "I'm Jewish in the same way the Olive Garden is an Italian restaurant. Which is to say: not very." He continues, "The closest my family came to observing Judaism was that paradoxical classic of assimilation: a Star of David on top of our Christmas tree"![2]

Jacobs decides to see what it would be like to live for an entire year by observing the Bible *literally*. "Millions of Americans say they take the Bible literally," he observes. But, "according to a 2005 Gallup poll, the number hovers near 33 percent; a 2004 *Newsweek* poll put it at 55 percent." What did Jacobs think?

> But my suspicion was that almost everyone's literalism consisted of picking and choosing. People plucked out the parts that fit their agenda, whether that agenda was to the right or to the left. Not me. I thought, with some naïveté, I would peel away the layers of interpretation and find the true Bible underneath. I would do this by being the ultimate fundamentalist. I'd be fearless. I would do exactly what the Bible said, and in so doing, I'd discover what's great and timeless in the Bible and what is outdated."[3]

For five hours each day over four months, Jacobs reads the whole Bible—from Genesis to Revelation. Every time he comes upon a commandment, he types it into his Apple PowerBook. (He's with the angels on that one!) Seventy-two pages long, more than seven hundred rules. As he reads, he realizes something if he practices every commandment: "All aspects of my life will be affected." He ruminates, "I'll be the Gandhi of the Upper West Side." Some will make him weird: "Bathe after sex. Don't eat the fruit from a tree planted less than five years ago.

Pay the wages of a worker every day." Some of the commandments are, in fact, banned by law: "Kill magicians." He's right: "This is going to be a monster project."[4]

You get the picture. If you want more, read his book. It's delightful. The whole book is a blue parakeet. It will make you rethink how we read the Bible.

What about Applying Jesus' Teachings Today?

I have no serious desire, though every now and then the idea does pass through my head just to see what it would be like, to observe all of Moses' laws "to the T." And I suspect 99.99 percent of you, if not more, stand alongside me in my lack of desire to do so. But I am quite willing to say that most of us do want to follow Jesus. Many of us, in fact, claim we do apply Jesus' teachings, literally to some degree, to everything we do.

Why talk about this? Because it is the *claim* that we follow Jesus alongside the obvious reality *that we don't follow Jesus completely* that leads us to *ponder how we are actually reading the Bible.* The passages we don't follow are blue parakeets that make us rethink how we read the Bible. All I really want to accomplish in this chapter is to get us to think more carefully about:

- the reality that we do pick and choose, even with Jesus and the New Testament, and
- the reasons we have for our adopting and adapting.

I've given away my secrets, of course, so let me state them clearly: we don't follow Jesus literally, we do pick and choose what we want to apply to our lives today, and I want to know what methods, ideas, and principles are at work among us for picking what we pick and choosing what we choose. Furthermore, it is my belief that *we—the church—have always read the Bible in a picking-and-choosing way. Somehow, someway we have formed patterns of discernment that guide us.*

Picking and choosing is how the church has always read the Bible! It is no doubt safer to call this "adapt and adopt." Whichever expression we use, it all comes down to one word: *discernment*. We have learned to discern how to live out the Bible in our world today; we have discerned what to do and what not to do, what to keep as permanent and what to see as "that was then." We do more than read and apply; we read, we listen, and we (in connection with God's Spirit and God's people) discern.

Perhaps your response to these claims is the same that asked of A. J. Jacobs: "Once you acknowledge that we pick and choose from the Bible, doesn't that destroy its credibility? Doesn't that knock the legs out from under it? Why should we put stock in any of the Bible?"[5] These are good questions, and many ask them. Just recently a student asked me those questions. But before any of us who claim to be Christians and who claim to follow Jesus can answer such questions, we need to look a little more closely at our practice of application. When we see how we actually live, we have two choices: either to become radical biblical literalists and apply everything (and I mean everything), or to admit that we are "pickers and choosers." Since the evidence reveals that we are all adopters and adapters, we need to admit it and then seek to explain ourselves. That is what this book attempts to do. I hope others will join the conversation.

I plan to give three examples from Jesus; we will explore other examples in the next chapter. I am tempted to go through example after example to bring out all the nuances, but that would make this book too long and detailed. In most examples, I do not even give my opinion. Instead, I am discussing how *we are already discerning* how to live the Bible and, in most cases, without much consciousness of what we are actually doing.

Jesus, Prayer, and Today

One day the disciples asked Jesus for some practical advice about prayer: "Lord," they said, "teach us to pray, just as John taught his disciples." In reply Jesus said to them (and I translate Jesus' words literally for effect): "*Whenever* you pray, *recite* this prayer …"; then he gives the shorter form of the Lord's Prayer (see Luke 11:1–4). The TNIV, emerging as it does from a world that does not believe in recited prayers, translates these words this way: "*When* you pray, *say…*" I have translated "when" with "whenever" as a more literal rendering of the Greek expression. And instead of "say," a more accurate rendering would be "recite." I do so because Luke uses a present imperative; Jesus expects this very prayer to be repeated over and over — *whenever* they pray. The best way to translate something that is said over and over is "recite."

TNIV	Literal
When you pray, say …	Whenever you pray, recite this…

Here is a fact from church history: to the best of our knowledge, the followers of Jesus have always recited the Lord's Prayer whenever they have gathered for worship and prayer. The evidence for this is universal — every major denomination in the world prior to the nineteenth and twentieth centuries recited the Lord's Prayer every Sunday. Why? Because Luke 11:2 taught them to do this. But most evangelical churches I have worshiped in and preached in do not recite the Lord's Prayer *whenever* they pray together. We have "applied" the words of Luke 11:2 differently, so differently that our translations reflect our own nonrecital of the Lord's Prayer. Why? Because there is an unwritten, contrary-to-what-Jesus-taught principle at work among us that reciting set prayers leads to vain repetitions.

I have no desire here to engage that debate. What needs to be realized is that this practice of *not reciting* the Lord's Prayer *whenever* we gather together is contrary to what Jesus said (and what the church has always done); rather, it is our *application of what Jesus said.*

We have chosen, for pastoral reasons, not to do what Jesus commanded us to do and have chosen instead to apply these words in another way. How? We take them as a *general principle* instead of a specific commandment, and this permits us to gather together in prayer without reciting the Lord's Prayer. This decision permits us to see the Lord's Prayer as a "model" prayer instead of a recited prayer. (For what it's worth, I think the Lord's Prayer is both a model and the precise words we should use *whenever* we gather in prayer. I recite it several times a day.)

Let's be honest: we treat this commandment of Jesus the way we treat most of the commands in Leviticus 19; that is, we ignore it or dismiss it.

Jesus, Conversion, and Today

As a second example, here is what Jesus requires or expects of those who want to enter the kingdom of heaven, all from the gospel of Matthew.

> They must have surpassing righteousness (Matthew 5:20).
> They must do God's will (7:21).
> They must become as a child in humility (18:3).
> They must cut themselves off from whatever is in the way (18:8–9).
> They must abandon riches (19:23–24).
> They must separate from the scribes and Pharisees (23:13).

How do we "apply" these so-called entrance requirements of Jesus? To anticipate, we mostly don't apply them. We have discerned what they meant and how to make use of them in our world.

For many Christians these statements by Jesus sound far too much like "works righteousness." That is, we prefer a similar kind of saying in John 3:3: "No one can see the kingdom of God without being born again." How is one "born again"? Many answer that from the same chapter, verse 15: "that everyone who believes may have eternal life in him."

But here's a question to think about: What would the gospel look like — in a four-point gospel tract — if we took the "abandon riches" call into the kingdom as the framework? How about this?

Point 1: God created the world for all of us.
Point 2: Some out of greed have established systemic injustices.
Point 3: Jesus calls us to abandon all of our riches to rectify this.
Point 4: If you abandon your riches, the kingdom will come and the world will be what God wants.

Most in the history of the church don't think that such a four-point gospel tract expresses the gospel. Some have thought more historically and see these entrance requirements as no more than concrete statements by Jesus to his fellow Jewish contemporaries who needed to hear those words in order to see what repentance and faith looked like. Regardless of what we do, in effect, if I may suggest so, we minimize what Jesus said in the list.

While I do think we can offer a more robust gospel than we do today,[6] the intent here is to get us to think about how we are reading the Bible. How do we know whether we are doing the right thing when, in effect, we suspend Jesus' concrete commands?

Jesus, Ethics, and Today

How do we apply Jesus' moral expectations? In particular, how do we apply the kinds of moral demands of Jesus we find in the Sermon on the Mount? We should be marked by a righteousness that (greatly) surpasses the righteousness of the Pharisees and teachers of the law (Matthew 5:20); we should avoid anger because Jesus teaches that anger is murderous (5:21–22); married folk should avoid lusting after others sexually because Jesus teaches that lust is adulterous (5:27–30); and we should, apart from the one singular exception in sexual infidelity, neither divorce nor remarry (5:31–32). To put all of this in one attractive container, we should be "perfect ... as your heavenly Father is perfect" (5:48). Even the disciples wondered if words like these were too much to handle; when Jesus said something similar sometime later, his best followers blurted out: "It is better not to marry!" (19:10).

How do we apply words like those in the Sermon on the Mount

today? Let's look at the different approaches in the history of the church to just one saying in this sermon: "Be perfect" (Matthew 5:48). What have we done with this statement of Jesus?

- Some say Jesus is exaggerating, raising the standard higher than we can achieve, but if we strive for it we'll do better than we are now.
- Others say that "being perfect" is what our moral life will be like in the eternal kingdom, and Jesus is teaching the final and eternal ethic God designs for us.
- Still others suggest that "being perfect" forces us to look inside to our heart of hearts to see our sinfulness.
- Yet others think Jesus means exactly what he says: he expects us to be perfect.
- One more: some think "perfect" actually means "whole" or "mature," so that being whole and mature is what Jesus really wants.

We will probably not agree on how to read the word "perfect" in Matthew 5:48, but I hope this little section gets us to think harder about how we are reading the Bible. We are not trying to resolve all these issues. Instead, we are intent on demonstrating that we apply some of what Jesus says and we choose not to apply other things Jesus has said. In other words, there is some adopting and adapting involved even with the sayings of Jesus. If there are two choices — totally literal or discerning a pattern — most of us will choose the latter every time.

By now I hope you are a bit unnerved about what I have said. This chapter is intended to provoke in order to get you to think together about *how you are actually reading the Bible.* Some of you may want to turn back to a much more literal, take-it-all-or-nothing approach, but I'm guessing most of you are now becoming aware that you do in fact adopt and adapt. What we must now discover is this: *What principles do we use to adopt and adapt the Bible?*

To answer this question we must broaden our vision from applying

Jesus' teachings to applying those of the whole Bible. When we do, we will discover that we use various patterns of *discernment*. In the next chapter we will go through seven more examples, each of which startles us Bible readers like the sudden appearance of a blue parakeet in the yard.

Chapter 10

Finding the Pattern
of Discernment

Why Do We *Not* Follow
the Bible Sometimes?

Our all-too-glib but rather frequently heard Christian claim to practice whatever the Bible says annoys me. You might be annoyed that
I have just said this, but I'd like a fair hearing. I ask you to consider
the following clear teachings of the Bible that few, if any, Christians
practice. Perhaps you can ask yourself this question as you read through
these passages: *Why do I* not *do what this passage in the Bible teaches?*

As you look at these examples, you will discover what I am calling
a *pattern of discernment.* The pattern of discernment is simply this: as
we read the Bible and locate each item in its place in the Story, as we
listen to God speak to us in our world through God's ancient Word,
we *discern — through God's Spirit and in the context of our community of
faith — a pattern of how to live **in our world.*** The church of every age
is summoned by God to the Bible to listen so we can discern a pattern
for living the gospel that is appropriate for our age. *Discernment* is part
of the process we are called to live.

DISCERNMENT:
General Thoughts

In general, I am thinking of what a *local church or a local denomination does in order to discern* how best to live out the gospel in its day and in its way. While personal discernment for my own life is important, that is not what I have in mind here. Instead, I am concerned with how a local church, often in deep conversation with a denomination, discerns how to live. In fact, often the discernment process occurs at the denominational level in order to guide each local church.

We do not need to get into all the ways various Christian churches make decisions. Rather, our concern in this book is about discernment at the local church level. Briefly put, Part 4 will probe how churches (locally or denominationally) make decisions about women in church ministries. A tension occurs when a young woman believes she is called to preach or teach publicly when a local church or denomination has "discerned" that to be unacceptable. The young woman's discernment is important to me, and I will deal with this, but our main concern is not so much with her discernment as with the church's discernment.

A second general issue concerns *diversity*. Every culture will discern its own patterns for living out the Bible. Turkish Christians will not discern the same pattern that Southern Californian Christians will discern. Russian Baptists will live out the gospel in ways that differ from Brasilian charismatics. Anglicans in India will discern in ways that differ from Anglicans in Wheaton. This is perhaps obvious to many, but we must remind ourselves of the vibrant diversity of the church when it comes to local level discernments. Seeking unanimity on all things is unwise; permitting discernment at the local level can sometimes create too much diversity, but it is wiser to have local discernment with some problems than having everyone under lock and key.

Furthermore, and I think this needs to be given special attention, the discernment can be very *messy*. Discernment is called for on issues that are obviously unclear in the Bible. No one discerns whether it is right to murder; no one believes spousal abuse is right; no one thinks selling off children is acceptable; and, in spite of the power of the question my reader asked in the previous chapter, most don't think premarital sexual intercourse is Christian behavior. These are clear and unmistakable teachings with which most Christians agree. This book is about the grey and fuzzy area called discernment.

Churches, for instance, do need to discern if they want women to preach on Sunday, and they will discern how gays and lesbians will participate. These are messy areas. Here's the rub: some revert to seeing the Bible as a law book to avoid the messiness. Eventually, though, a day will come when it becomes clear that some discernment is going on. That's what I'm most concerned about in this book.

DISCERNMENT:
Specific Examples

Let's look at some examples — some of them quite messy — and we will learn about the unstated principle of discernment at work in the church.

1. Divorce and Remarriage

Let me make five quick observations to get in our minds what we mean by discernment in divorce and remarriage.[1] First, Jesus was against divorce, as is clear from Mark 10:11–12: "Anyone who divorces his wife and marries another woman commits adultery against her. And if she divorces her husband and marries another man, she commits adultery."

Second, on another occasion Jesus "discerned" there is, in fact, an exception — sexual immorality.[2] Look at Matthew 5:32: "But I tell you that anyone who divorces his wife, *except for sexual immorality*, causes her to become an adulteress, and anyone who marries the divorced woman commits adultery" (emphasis added). Now we've got clarity: divorce is wrong except in the case of sexual immorality.

Third, the apostle Paul encountered a new situation in which he had to *discern* how the teachings of Jesus could be lived out when a non-Christian spouse deserted a Christian spouse. Was divorce also permissible for this situation? In 1 Corinthians 7, Paul discerned it was permissible. Paul knew precisely what he was doing—adding to what Jesus had taught. In 7:12 he says: "To the rest I say this (I, not the Lord)." What did he discern? "But if the unbeliever leaves, let it be so. The brother or sister is not bound in such circumstances; God has called us to live in peace" (7:15).

True to Jesus, Paul is not looking for exceptions. He prefers that husband and wife stay together because the Christian might "save" the partner (7:16). But, if the nonbeliever deserts, Paul discerns divorce is permissible, and he does so because we are called "to live in peace," which probably means Paul wants the Christians not to be disruptive in society.

Now the fourth point: churches are called to enact similar discernments today, and long, hard, prayerful sessions have been directed at discerning whether abuse and desertion and immaturities are permissible grounds for divorce even among Christians. This is the messy part. No one says it is easy, but we have the following confidences: the guidance of the Spirit is promised us as we pray, as we study Scripture, and as we join in the conversation *with* church tradition. It would be much easier for God to have given us rules and regulations for everything. But God, in his wisdom, has chosen not to do that. Discernment is an element of what it means to walk by faith.

Fifth, I believe our discernments should never become *rules or laws*. The moment we turn our discernments into rules or the moment we elevate them to the level of official positions, they are headed in the direction of fossilization, inflexibility, and the near impossibility of rethinking, renewing, and reforming. We'll soon have a Lucca wall around our Bible. Instead, we need to render discernments with all the wisdom we can muster and let them remain as discernments and judgments.

In our discussion of examples below we will find some patterns at work in our discernment, but these are not rules we apply; rather, they are discernments. I am nervous about anyone who thinks we can find a mechanism that will guide our path. Instead, we need attentiveness to the Spirit as we read the Bible together and to the guiding of the Spirit.

I accept the reality that churches already disagree over discernments. I also accept the reality that the process will be difficult. And I accept the reality that even within a church where a sensitive process of discernment has been followed, there will be folks who disagree. That's the way it is, and it is also the way the church has always read the Bible. Longing for a day of certainty in this life may propel us into deeper discussions and the search for greater unity, but certainty and unanimity in discernment are not the world in which we live.

What the New Testament trajectory teaches us about divorce and remarriage is the need to remain firmly committed to marriage while permitting divorce in cases where the marital covenant has been destroyed. The pattern is to discern *the underlying reason for the fractured relationship and then to judge if that reason is acceptable.*

2. Circumcision

God told Abraham to make the covenant between them official by circumcising every male child *forever.* We need to read all these verses to see how serious this circumcision issue was:

> Then God said to Abraham, "As for you, you must keep my covenant, you and your descendants after you *for the generations to come.* This is my covenant with you and *your descendants after you,* the covenant you are to keep: *Every* male among you shall be circumcised. You are to undergo circumcision, and it will be the sign of the covenant between me and you. *For the generations to come* every male among you who is eight days old must be circumcised, including those born in your household or bought with money from a foreigner — those who are not your offspring. Whether

born in your household or bought with your money, they must be circumcised. My covenant in your flesh is to be *an everlasting covenant.* Any uncircumcised male, who has not been circumcised in the flesh, will be cut off from his people; he has broken my covenant." (Genesis 17:9–14, emphasis added)

Circumcision had been a big deal for the Jewish community for centuries. For this reason converts to Judaism were required to undergo circumcision. It was therefore natural for Jewish followers of Jesus to expect Gentile converts to go all the way and go under the knife for Jesus (Acts 15). The question of whether converts should be circumcised was the pressing question that "cut like a knife" through the early churches. Think of this like a debate room with each party sitting together facing the other and a large group of undecideds surrounding both groups. Here are the options:

Pharisee-type Christians:	"By all means! Circumcision is God's command."
Pauline Christians:	"No, the times have changed!"
Undecided group:	"What should we do?"

The early Christians were at a stalemate. To deal with their differences and discern how to live, they convened the first church conference in Jerusalem, where there were no doubt plenty of knives under the tunics of the Pharisaic side to complete their deliberations.

What we find in Acts 15 is *the pattern of discernment.* The early Christians discerned that circumcision, the *(don't forget this)* ageless command to Abraham, was not necessary for Gentile converts. James, brother of Jesus and now leader of the church in Jerusalem, came to the conclusion that Gentile converts were like "resident aliens" and needed only to offer a minimal respect for those commandments that had always distinguished the Jews from the surrounding nations (15:16–21). Here we find a pattern of discernment, a pattern of listening to the old, understanding the present, and discerning how to live that old way in a new day.

But ... what was decided in Jerusalem wasn't enough for Paul, who developed his own pattern of discernment for his churches. In fact, Paul went further than James with *three modifications of the Old Testament commandment to circumcise every boy forever.* First, in one of the most radical positions Paul ever took, he said *circumcision really didn't matter*: "For in Christ Jesus neither circumcision nor uncircumcision has any value. The only thing that counts is faith expressing itself through love" (Galatians 5:6). I don't know how that strikes you, but it doesn't take a professional historian to imagine how Paul's opponents and Jewish friends would have responded. Paul's opponents knew with certainty that Paul was disagreeing with God's Word! In terms of this book, Paul's statement was a blue parakeet observation, and this whole book converges right here. How did Paul discern that circumcision didn't really matter?

Second, drawing on a theme in Moses and Jeremiah, Paul argued that *circumcision, even in the Old Testament, was ultimately an image of the heart* and not simply surgery on the body. Thus, Moses says in Deuteronomy 10:16: "Circumcise your hearts, therefore, and do not be stiff-necked any longer." And Jeremiah 4:4 says: "Circumcise yourselves to the LORD, circumcise your hearts, you people of Judah and inhabitants of Jerusalem." Paul puts it like this: "A person is not a Jew who is one only outwardly, nor is circumcision merely outward and physical. No, a person is a Jew who is one *inwardly*; and *circumcision is circumcision of the heart, by the Spirit, not by the written code*" (Romans 2:28–29, emphasis added).

If this didn't confuse some of Paul's criticisms what about this? "Circumcision is nothing and uncircumcision is nothing. Keeping God's commands is what counts" (1 Corinthians 7:19). His opponents would have said like the duck on the TV commercial, "AFLAC! (Isn't circumcision one of those commandments?)" For Paul, circumcision was clearly a commandment of God for all time, but, paradoxically, it was now no longer necessary for those who were "in Christ" because real circumcision was a matter of the heart. Which means circumcision is forever but it morphs from a physical to a spiritual act. (You're not alone if you think Moses would have muttered and shook his head when Paul said these things.)

And third, Paul went one step further: *baptism fulfills and replaces circumcision*. Notice these words from Colossians 2:11 – 12: "In him you were also circumcised with a circumcision not performed by human hands. Your sinful nature was put off when you were circumcised by Christ, having been buried with him in baptism, in which you were also raised with him through your faith in the working of God, who raised him from the dead." We might argue, then, that for Paul circumcision was eternal because it morphed into baptism.

We who are Christians today no longer circumcise for reasons of the covenant because what was at one time expressed as a universal, eternal commandment was understood by early Christians — *in a pattern of Spirit-led discernment* — to be an external rite that would eventually find its fulfillment in the Christian rite of baptism. By the time Paul was done with this Old Testament commandment, the knives of circumcision were, to play with his terms, tossed into the water. So, should we practice circumcision? No. Why not? Because we believe circumcision was a temporary entrance requirement that found fulfillment in baptism. And we believe this because we believe the Spirit who told Abraham to circumcise also told the early Christians that the day of circumcision had come to an end. The pattern of discernment can be called *theological development*. In other words, "that theology was then, but this theology is now."

I wish examples like this were all so clear. They're not.

3. The Style of Christian Women

Wives, in the same way submit yourselves to your own husbands so that, if any of them do not believe the word, they may be won over without words by the behavior of their wives, when they see the purity and reverence of your lives. Your beauty should not come from outward adornment, such as elaborate hairstyles and the wearing of gold jewelry and fine clothes. Rather, it should be that of your inner self, the unfading beauty of a gentle and quiet spirit, which is of great worth in God's sight. For this is the way the holy women of the past who put their hope in God used to adorn themselves. They submitted themselves to their own husbands, like Sarah, who obeyed Abraham and called him her lord. You are her daughters if you do what is right and do not give way to fear.

This text, from 1 Peter 3:1–6, contains three basic commands to women in first-century Asia Minor who had unbelieving husbands. They should:

- submit to their non-Christian husbands in order to convert them.
- avoid elaborate hairstyles and gold jewelry and fine clothing.
- address their husbands with the word "lord."

Even if some conservative Christians today want to emphasize wives submitting to their husbands no matter how countercultural it may seem, they don't usually insist on Peter's commands about elaborate hair and nice clothing and fine jewelry, and they don't, so far as I know, insist on their calling their husbands "lord."

Why do we not follow these explicit words of the apostle Peter? The only answer I can give is that over time the church has worked out a pattern of discernment that comes to this: women (and men I might add) should dress modestly. Even this pattern is not entirely accurate; for some the pattern of discernment is more radical. For them Peter's words are simply passé and outmoded. "That was then, but this is now. Peter's words are 'then,'" Many Christian women dress in the most fashionable clothing, pay considerable fees for coiffure, and have no qualms about expensive jewelry. Furthermore, they wear such things to church on Sunday morning where everyone can see them and where, by and large, no one puts up a fuss. I will avoid any sense of judgment on this matter.

What I am curious about is the pattern of discernment we now use. Let's say that we think Peter's intent is to encourage Christian women to be modest. My question, then, is this: How do we discern that his intent can be reduced to the principle of modesty instead of timeless commands? This pattern of discernment might be called *the deeper principle*. This approach knows that the principle is transcultural but the specific expressions of that principle are not.

Let's press on.

4. Sun-Centered or Earth-Centered Cosmology

The Bible assumes that the earth was the center of the universe, but we now know, in spite of the strife it caused Galileo and the backpedaling required of the church since his days, that the sun is at the center of the solar system. Our cosmology is helio-centric (sun-centered) whereas the Bible's is geo-centric (earth-centered). Frequently the Bible speaks of the earth's foundation. The earth, the biblical authors say, sits atop a stable foundation with pillars: "He shakes the earth from its place and makes its pillars tremble" (Job 9:6; see 38:4–7; Proverbs 8:27–29). As if assuming the earth is flat, the biblical authors speak of its four corners. So, for example, the seer of Revelation says: "After this I saw four angels standing at the four corners of the earth, holding back the four winds of the earth to prevent any wind from blowing on the land or on the sea or on any tree" (Revelation 7:1).

In the biblical perception of the world, we have a principle at work we must admit: God spoke in those days in those ways, and some of those ways were a three-deckered universe of below the earth, the earth, and the heavens (see 1 Peter 3:19–22). I suspect that's how they thought the world was really constructed.

How do we deal with a geo-centric, flat-earth, and three-layered universe? Science, which now factors into our patterns of discernment, rules for most of us, and we revise our view of what the Bible is actually saying. We have discerned that the Bible is actually using "phenomenological" language—language that expresses what the ancients observed, heard, and felt. Their language, then, is metaphorical. Are we bound to think that because the Bible implies the earth is flat and rests on pillars with a foundation that the earth is flat and sits on pillars? Some do, but most of us adjust and take the Bible with us into our modern, scientific world.

Most of us also believe that what we thought the Bible was saying is not, in fact, what it was saying. The pattern of discernment here is simply *growth in knowledge, scientific and otherwise.* It need only to be mentioned that some think the same scientific development can be applied, say, to Genesis 1 and 2, while others want to stop short of such an implication. I am much less concerned to take a stance on such issues and more concerned to admit that such a pattern of discernment is at work. Some of us are willing to give it more freedom than others.

5. The Death Penalty

Here we walk on thinner ice or into a more-debated issue. Some Christians, *knowing full well what the Old Testament says and knowing that Romans 13 might be sanctioning death sentences,* believe that Christians should not support capital punishment. They believe a better way is possible for our world. For such persons, prosecution and life in prison is enough. Who knows, they ask, if this person might be reconciled to God, restored by grace, and made anew?

There are all kinds of texts and issues that come to play. Here are just a few: the Old Testament sanctioned capital punishment for the witch (Exodus 22:18), the idolater (22:20), the blasphemer (Leviticus 24:13), the rebellious son (Deuteronomy 21:18 – 21), adultery (22:22), and the one who broke Sabbath (Numbers 15:32 – 36).

There are, however, some other tendencies and trends. Cain was not put to death for murdering his brother (Genesis 4). There were cities of refuge where someone guilty of unintentional murder was both protected from blood revenge but yet somehow confined (Exodus 21:12 – 14; Numbers 35:6 – 34; Deuteronomy 4:41 – 43; 19:1 – 13). Importantly, the guilty person in a city of refuge (analogous to our prisons) was released when the reigning high priest died (Numbers 35:25). Furthermore, Jesus didn't demand capital punishment for the woman caught in adultery (John 7:53 – 8:11).[3] Even more important, Jesus may well have undercut the foundation for capital punishment when he demanded that his followers turn the other cheek (Matthew 5:38–39).

On top of the Bible, humans have done centuries of thinking about deterrence—does capital punishment actually deter crime? They think about protection—doesn't a criminal's death make for a safer society? They think about life—doesn't capital punishment demonstrate the value of life? They think about money—isn't it cheaper to put some away than pay for their life confinement? They think about statistics—does not capital punishment weigh more heavily for the poor than for the wealthy who can afford lawyers? They think about problems—we know some on death row have been proven innocent. Doesn't that force us to rethink the whole system? I could go on.

The fundamental argument against capital punishment goes something like this: "that was then, but this is now." Christians are split on this one. Jesus' teachings unleashed a new system of grace and forgiveness. In addition, society has developed in law, in enforcement, and in restoration to such a degree that capital punishment is no longer needed. The pattern of discernment for those who oppose capital punishment combines *social progress, historical development, legal development, and theological development that climaxes in Jesus' own teachings.* Furthermore, that development continues into our own day.

6. Tongues

Our sixth example is tongue speaking, more often now called by its Greek term *glossalalia.* Here are the simple facts: the early Christians spoke in tongues (Acts 2), Paul spoke in tongues frequently (1 Corinthians 14:18), and Christians throughout the church have spoken in tongues (names omitted). But, and here's the important point, since most Christians don't speak in tongues, because in the history of the church most haven't spoken in tongues, and because tongue speaking was often isolated into small pockets of Christians, a pattern of discernment arose that "tongues aren't for today, they were a sign gift of the first century." And the pattern of "that was then, but this is now" was fine until the Pentecostal movement in the early 1900s, the charismatic movement of the 1960s, and the Vineyard movement of the 1970s and 1980s. At that time the "pattern" was discerned as a "no longer not for us" pattern. In other words, "that was then, but this is now" became a "that was then, and it is also now" pattern.

What we have here is a *variation in contexts*. Some think *glossalalia* was a manifestation of God's Spirit at the birth of the church but is no longer a pattern for the church. Others, however, find a *normative pattern of discernment*: *glossalalia* is a permanent gift of the Spirit to the church. As a seminary student I routinely rode to school with a fellow seminarian who was Assembly of God. Often we chatted about charismatic gifts, and I will never forget what he said to me when I asked why I didn't speak in tongues but he did — and that everyone around him did and that no one around me did. His answer: "Those who grow up *with it* are more likely to speak in tongues." Evidence backs him up, whether we like it or not. Those who grow up with tongues are more likely to speak in tongues. Variations in context, then, reveal to us that our own context shapes in part not only our interpretations but also our practices.

It is not my intent to resolve this issue either. Instead, we conclude on an important note: *the pattern of discernment varies from age to age and from church to church and from person to person within a church.* This illustrates that the pattern of discernment can sometimes be messy.

We have two options:

uniformity of all in all things, or (which is what we really have) diversity in the striving for unity.

This is precisely what Paul means by the verses in our final example.

7. All Things to All

First Corinthians 9:19–23 reads as follows:

Though I am free and belong to no one, I have made myself a slave to everyone, to win as many as possible. To the Jews I became like a Jew, to win the Jews. To those under the law I became like one under the law (though I myself am not under the law), so as to win those under the law. To those not having the law I became like one not having the law (though I am not free from God's law but am under Christ's law), so as to win those not having the law. To the weak I became weak, to win the weak. I have become all things to all people so that by all possible means I might save some. I do all this for the sake of the gospel, that I may share in its blessings.

Paul's adaptability to context has drawn attention. Gordon Fee, a New Testament scholar, speaks of Paul's "apparently chameleonlike stance in matters of social relationships."[4] The apostle began a sermon to philosopher types by exploring the gospel in philosophical terms (Acts 17:16–34). When it came to traditional Jewish food laws, he evidently just turned his head (see 1 Corinthians 8; also, written later, Romans 14:2–3, 6). Why did Paul do this? Because of the gospel. If one wants to be completely faithful to Paul today, one would have to submit every act and every idea to the principle of what furthers the gospel the most. Because of that principle, Paul adopted and adapted.

Yes, Paul was a chameleon — he changed colors everywhere he went — but he kept the same body. His gospel mission shaped everything he did. His gospel was the same, but his circumstances shaped how we went about his business of spreading the gospel. Paul's process was messy to outsiders but Spirit-led to insiders.

Some are a bit taken aback by Paul, but reading the Bible as Story makes me think Paul is doing nothing new here. Adaptability of message and lifestyle is a theme written into the fabric of the ongoing development of the Bible itself. God spoke in:

Abraham's days in Abraham's ways (walking between severed animals)
Moses' days in Moses' ways (law and ceremony)
David's days in David's ways (royal policies)
Isaiah's days in Isaiah's ways (walking around nude for a few years)

Ezra's days in Ezra's ways (divorcing Gentile spouses)
Jesus' days in Jesus' ways (intentional poverty)
Peter's days in Peter's ways (strategies for living under an emperor)
John's days in John's ways (dualistic language—light and darkness)

Adaptability and development are woven into the very fabric of the Bible. From beginning to end there is a pattern of adopting and adapting. It is the attempt to foist one person's days and ways on everyone's days and ways that quenches the Holy Spirit. Can we be biblical if we fail to be as adaptable as the Bible itself was—only for our world? Is this messy? Sometimes it is. Was the Jerusalem council messy? Yes, it was. Did they discern what to do for that time? Yes, they did. Was it permanent, for all time, for everyone, always, everywhere? No.

All genuine biblical faith takes the gospel message and "incarnates" it in a context. So, we lay down this observation that unmasks all that we are advocating:

What is good for Abraham, Moses, David, Isaiah, Ezra, Jesus, Peter, and Paul is also good for us. But, the precise expression of the gospel or the manner of living of Abraham, Moses, David, Isaiah, Ezra, Jesus, Peter, and Paul may not be our expression or our manner of living. Living out the Bible means living out the Bible in our day in our way by discerning together how God would have us live.

We can be firmer: it is unlikely, since it is clear that each of these persons adapted the Plot and the Story for their day, that their message or manner of life will be precisely the same as our message and our manner of life. We are called, as they were, to learn the Plot and the Story, to listen to God, and to discern what to say and how to live in our day in our own way. We will speak to our world only when we unleash the gospel so that it can speak *in our day in our ways*. But we are called to be faithful, and we do this by staying on the slide—by reading the Bible and knowing the Bible and living out its story in our world today.

What this book is advocating is not new. It is my belief that most

Christians and churches do operate with a pattern of discernment, but it is rarely openly admitted and even more rarely clarified. Discernment, I am arguing, is how we have always read the Bible; in fact, it is how the biblical authors themselves read the Bible they had! I want to begin a conversation among Bible readers about this very topic: What pattern of discernment is at work among us?

I want now to dig a little deeper into one example: women in church ministries. I am not asking you to agree with me in the next few chapters, but I am asking you to admit that everyone today is using a pattern of discernment when it comes to women in church ministries. Passages in the Bible about women are blue parakeet passages. Let me play with that metaphor by asking you a question: Are we silencing the blue parakeets (women today) by ignoring blue parakeet passages about women? Or, are we silencing the women of the Bible by silencing blue parakeet passages about women?

The next few chapters will illustrate what it means to read the Bible *with* tradition instead of reading the Bible *through* tradition. In essence, I think the church has gotten off track, misread some passages in the Bible, ignored others, and then fossilized that reading of the Bible into the Great Tradition. While I respect that tradition, I have learned that reading the Bible *with* tradition encourages each generation to think for itself by returning to the Bible, confessing the Bible's primacy, and unleashing the power of the gospel in our day in our way.

Part 4

Women in Church Ministries Today

A Case Study in Rethinking How You Read the Bible

There is neither Jew nor Gentile, neither slave nor free, neither male nor female, for you are all one in Christ Jesus.

The apostle Paul, according to Galatians 3:28

I have become all things to all people so that by all possible means I might save some. I do all this for the sake of the gospel, that I may share in its blessings.

The apostle Paul, according to 1 Corinthians 9:22–23

When I was a professor at Trinity Evangelical Divinity School (TEDS) from 1983 to 1995, the debate about women in church ministries was one of the hot topics. In writing here about "women in church ministries," I want to emphasize that I am not talking only about senior pastors and elders and preaching and teaching from pulpits on Sunday mornings, but about anything God calls women to do. Much of the debate about women in ministry, of course, revolves around the word "ordination" and senior pastors and public preaching. But we have a wider scope than that kind of ministry.

As a young professor, I made two decisions — one of them subtle and which I regret, and one of them enduring and about to be documented in the next few chapters. The subtle decision I regret is that, because the issues around TEDS were so inflammatory and anyone who thought otherwise about women was held either as theologically liberal or intellectually suspect, I made the decision not to enter into the public debate. Class preparation and some other writing projects, besides a young family and an income that didn't make life anything other than a monthly chase, did not give me the time to be proficient enough to enter the fray. (I now wish I had.) But, I listened and learned from what I was hearing.

The discussion itself led me into many hours of thinking and deliberating with students, but only rarely with colleagues. What I concluded then was that I simply didn't read the Bible the way those who opposed women in church ministries, especially teaching and leading ministries, did. Some of the public debaters have the habit of calling anyone who moves in a different direction a liberal and at times have the other habit of showing that those who differ must be denying inerrancy. Some announce that those who differ with the traditional view are on a slippery slope into theological liberalism. Beside the fact that most slippery slopes aren't very slippery and neither are they slopes cascading into liberalism, the facts are against this announcement. Many who do disagree with the traditional view are not in fact liberals. I could give you a list of them. Most of them are card-carrying evangelicals. I am one of them.

What I realized as I listened to the debates was that I read the Bible as Story (though that was not the term I was using at that time), and I thought (and still think) that many of the traditionalists read the Bible as a law book and a puzzle. Perhaps a gentler way of putting this is to suggest that I think traditionalists read the Bible about women in church ministries *through* tradition instead of reading the Bible *with* tradition. The latter challenges the tradition while the former does not. It is always safer to read the Bible *through* tradition. In this instance, the tradition got it wrong. Now, before I get to a sketch of the view I now believe to be more biblical and one that encourages us to expand the ministries of women, I want to sketch where I have come from.

How I Changed My Mind

Fundamentalism

I grew up in a fundamentalist Christian home and church in the Midwest. Our home was traditional in this sense: my father and mother lived their lives within what might be called traditional roles. My father was a public school teacher; my mother a housewife until my sisters and I were old enough for her to begin working to supplement the income. My mother was (and still is) an ambitious and talented woman who, had she been born thirty years later, would have become a successful businessperson or leader of some kind. My father called the shots but my mother ran the place, though I can't say I paid much attention to such things. I absorbed this way of living as natural.

Our church was also traditionalist. We had no women in any kind of public ministry other than my mother, who was the choir director. I am reasonably certain no woman ever preached from our pulpit, though women did sing and give testimonies. The one exception might be female missionaries who came through at times to report on their missionary efforts. They did not preach or teach; rather, they gave witness or reports. The difference between teaching and giving witness was important, even if mistaken.

However, the windows were slightly open in our fundamentalist church because one of our neighbors, Dorothy Libby, was a Sunday school teacher for young adults — post-high-school, college-age adults — even though she was a woman. She loved to study the Bible, had a mind of her own, read what was available in commentaries, books, and Bible dictionaries, and overall did something that technically was against the silent code—women were not to teach male adults.

Education

I went off to a fundamentalist Christian college, where the same ideas were present. I had a brilliant Western lit teacher named Diana Portfleet, who had a keen perception of theology and church history, but she did not teach Bible or theology. Dr. Portfleet at some level opened the window for me even more. I do not recall women in church ministries being an issue for me either when I was in college or, as a student at TEDS, when I was in seminary.

During my doctoral days in England this issue came up in a variety of ways, and while my recollection is that I was a quiet traditionalist with more than a willingness to think about the problems, my own intellectual interests were about other topics. I was focused on gospel studies and how Judaism worked. But one day riding my bicycle in Cambridge, England, I observed that the person riding a bicycle next to me was none other than Professor Morna Hooker, the great Methodist New Testament scholar at Cambridge University. In an odd sort of way my heart was strangely warmed.

After exchanging pleasantries and fighting off the temptation to engage in nonstop prattle with her as we rode together across Cambridge, something occurred to me that opened my own window more. I realized how much I had learned from Morna Hooker's exquisite and insightful scholarship. Most importantly, this moment of bicycle riding with her drove me to the conclusion that anyone who thinks it is wrong for a woman to teach in a church can be consistent with that point of view only if they refuse to read and learn from women scholars. This means not reading their books lest they become teachers.

Some people think it is pedantic to equate reading-to-learn with a teaching ministry. I don't, and I stand by it until someone can convince me that reading-to-learn is different from listening-to-learn. Right then and there, while riding on a bicycle next to Professor Hooker, I became convinced that teaching is teaching and learning is learning, that reading her books was learning from her, and that the times have changed. If men could learn from a woman scholar's writings about theology and the Bible, if men could learn from a New Testament expert who gave substance to their (male) sermons and ideas and theology, then they were being taught—call it what you want—by a woman.

Teaching

So, by the time I began teaching at TEDS, while I cannot say that my mind was clear in all regards or that I had become consistent in my own head, I can say that the genesis of change was in the past. I was a traditionalist at some level, but all I needed was an opportunity. Teaching students, especially women, became that opportunity. The window was not thrown open all at once. My change was gradual, and what most changed it was the study of the New Testament and that realization that I believed that the New Testament—all of it—*emerged from and therefore was shaped by* first-century Jewish and Greco-Roman culture, including what it said about women. Within a year or two I had become convinced that the traditionalist view was misreading and misusing the Bible. I taught at TEDS for more than a decade. Apart from classroom discussions, I did not get into these issues in public.

As I was writing this interlude, which has led to some soul-searching, I read through what I wrote on Galatians 3:28 and 1 Peter 3:1–6 in my commentaries on those books—one passage about "neither male nor female" and the other passage about women submitting to their unbelieving spouse.[1] Those commentaries were written as I was making the transition from TEDS to North Park University, and they were also the first time I went public with my views. In both commentaries I sketched how I thought we should read the Bible—as a culturally conditioned revelation of God's Word that needs to be worked out in a modern context. My own views have developed since then, but the foundational argument was present in both commentaries. I regret now that I did not engage traditionalists at that time, even though the views I was taking at that time gave me a foundation to engage in that debate.

In the process of being interviewed to teach at North Park, two of my future colleagues, Sonia Bodi and Nancy Arnesen, took me to coffee. Nancy, a gentle, fair-minded woman and one firmly entrenched in a Christian feminist perspective, asked me my view of women in church ministries. I won't forget what I said: "I'm for women in ministry," I answered.

"But what about Paul?" she asked back.

To cut to the chase I said, "Paul's directions to his churches were culturally shaped." We spent time discussing that point of view. The window was open for me (and so was a teaching post I love).

Before I go on, I must also confess that I know and believe that I (and my colleagues) failed our female students at TEDS, that we should have engaged this debate "tooth and claw," and that had we done so the Evangelical Free Church as well as that seminary may have been a much more liberating institution than it is today. I want to confess to the many female students that we (and I) were wrong and I am asking you to forgive us (and me). I can only hope the recent hire of a woman in theology will lead to more women on the TEDS faculty. I also hope such appointments come with an official confession and invited response by former women students.

I have loads of respect for my friends and colleagues at TEDS, not the least of whom were my teachers: Walt Liefeld and Grant Osborne. Both Walt and Grant took a stand for women's ordination against the grain at TEDS and helped me in many ways to see the light on this issue, but none of us fought the battle as fiercely as was required for the time. I don't want to make it look as if I was simmering or seething under a tightly stopped-up lid of oppression. I could have done more; we could have done more. Walt and Grant did far more than I did.

Finally, I want to call attention to the many women students we had who endured traditionalist teachers. Unintentionally or intentionally, these women were suppressed from exercising their gifts and have been barred from ministries—some of whom, to my great delight, like Sarah Sumner and Alice Shirey, have found their way into careers of teaching, speaking, pastoring, and writing while others have had to pursue other careers—in spite of a calling from God to teach and preach.

Since I've mentioned Sarah and Alice, I also want to mention two outstandingly gifted women who have never found a sacred space among evangelicals, Cheryl Hatch and Jane Goleman. These two women, and I could mention others, were some of the best students I have ever taught and some of the most gifted. But their own commitments to evangelicalism have kept them among evangelicals who, sadly, silence blue parakeets.

I want to tell more of Cheryl's story, but that will begin our next chapter.

Chapter 11

The Bible and Women

Women in Church Ministries 1

In one of my early classes of teaching at TEDS I had a fantastic student named Cheryl Hatch. She had already flourished for a decade as a campus minister with "Crusade" (her name for Campus Crusade for Christ, a ministry to college students); she had a firm grasp of both the Bible and Christian theology; she had exceptional interpersonal skills; her mature faith was obvious. In my class of "exegeting" 1 Peter, each student was assigned to summarize how they would preach a given passage. Cheryl's "sermonette" stood above — head and shoulders — the others in the class. Not only was Cheryl mature in faith and competent theologically, she was also gifted to preach.

But when Cheryl graduated with her Master of Arts in Religion with an emphasis in New Testament, she could find no church willing to call her as a preaching or teaching pastor. Why? Very simple: she was an evangelical *but* she was a woman. She received offers to serve as a children's pastor or a youth pastor or a women's ministry pastor, but no church — zero — even considered her to stand behind a pulpit on Sunday morning to preach the gospel and expound the Bible, *even though she was gifted and competent and willing* and felt God had called her to do so.

The irony of this now haunts me. Cheryl was a gifted evangelist. One moment's reflection on the significance of evangelism, from which gift (to my knowledge) women have never been barred, should lead us to some about-face changes. If a woman is given the freedom to explain the gospel and persuade others to respond to the gospel, and if the message of evangelism shapes how a person will eventually live as a Christian, consistency would demand that we either bar women from evangelism or permit them to teach and preach as well. Anyone, so I would say, who permits women to evangelize ought to permit them to preach; after all, what is "preaching" in the New Testament if it does not include evangelism?

Cheryl returned to Washington, DC, where to this day she enjoys a full life of federal employment, participates actively in her local church, and perseveres in the ongoing development of her own theological studies. Kris and I remain friends to this day with Cheryl, and she appears to harbor no bitterness toward those who have not permitted her to exercise her gifts. I am willing to say now that the evangelical church missed out on someone who could have been a dynamic pastor.

Let me now return to my image: Cheryl was a blue parakeet; blue parakeets, the church was saying at the time she was "on the market," are to remain in their cages and to keep silent. Are they? Let's look again at the Bible and I will show you in the next few chapters how many have discerned what we are to do today with blue parakeets, women, who think they are called to sing and fly in the ministries of the church. I will argue that we should let the blue parakeets sing, that in reading the Bible *with* tradition instead of *through* tradition, we are set free both to respect and challenge that tradition. Furthermore, the direction of the Bible itself encourages us to think of facing the future by expanding the church ministries of women.

In this and the next few chapters we will offer a positive argument for why we think the Bible affirms the ongoing presence of women in church ministries. We will look at a variety of topics, including a quick sweep through the whole Bible to show how the Bible as Story informs our reading of these passages. Any discussion that defends women in church ministries can be responsible only if it examines in more detail the so-called silencing of women passages in Paul (1 Corinthians 14:34–35 and 1 Timothy 2:8–15). So, we will have to slow down our pace a little to examine those two passages in our final chapters.

However, I must ask for your sympathy about one point: in this book it is impossible to discuss all the issues and all the counterarguments about this debated issue of women in church ministries. I will not even try to do this, nor will I sketch the views of those who are traditionalists in these matters. There are other books that do that. Our book is merely illustrating how we read the Bible—story, listen, discern—by offering women in church ministries as a test case. Could more be said? Yes. I am deeply aware of the many, many issues I would like to bring up, and maybe at a later time I will develop this discussion at more length; but for now I offer the next few chapters as an example of how to read the Bible as Story, to learn how to listen, and to discern how to live the Bible in our world.

I'd like to begin this discussion by looking at this point: "that was then, but this is now."

Similar but Shifting Contexts

It is customary for those who favor women in church ministries to begin with an infamous prayer of the rabbis and then to make it clear that neither Jesus nor the early Christians saw women this way. Then such persons usually suggest that Jesus and Christianity "liberated" women from an oppressive world, and they walk away feeling a little morally superior for the progress we have made. I will also include this prayer that everyone refers to, but I want to emphasize that this rabbinic statement tells only a part of the story of women in Judaism and the biblical world. We should not forget the Song of Songs when it comes to what women thought of men and men of women! Still, the social conditions giving rise to this prayer are a real part of the ancient world—the part that reveals that women were considered unequal and in some cases inferior to men.

R. Judah says, "A man must recite three benedictions every day:

Praised be Thou, O Lord, who did not make me a gentile;
Praised be Thou, O Lord, who did not make me a boor;
Praised be Thou, O Lord, who did not make me a woman."

Why did the rabbis say this of women? Because "women are not obligated [to perform all] the commandments."[1] So, the budding rabbi is to give thanks to God because, as a male, he gets to observe all the commandments while a woman, for a variety of reasons—not the least being menstruation—is not so privileged. I don't believe this is what Jewish men thought of women in general. Some men? To be sure. All men? No. Moreover, this prayer may have been a Jewish version of an ancient Greek saying. Thus, the Greek male is taught to be grateful "that I was born a human being and not a beast, next, a man and not a woman, thirdly, a Greek and not a barbarian."[2]

So, in general, what was it like for women in the Jewish world? Worse than today; sometimes much, much worse; sometimes just worse. But still worse. Statements about women in the Bible, like the story of Jephthah in Judges 11, may strike us today like a blue parakeet we'd like to tame, but we dare not. Instead, we must look these passages in the eye, let them be what they are, and embrace them as part of the Bible's story. Only then can we learn that reading the Bible as Plot and Story enables us to see how these texts fit in an ongoing story of "that was then, but this is now." So, a few points about the Bible and women.

He Who Writes the Story . . .

We must say something not often admitted by Bible-reading, God-loving Christians: He who writes the story controls the glory. What's the point? The Bible was written by men, and the Bible tells stories from the angle of men. We admit this because we admit that God spoke in those days in those ways, and those days and those ways were male days and male ways. Mary J. Evans, a female professor of Old Testament at the evangelical London Bible College, wrote the essays on "Women" in the evangelical dictionaries from InterVarsity Press called *Dictionary of the Old Testament: Pentateuch* and the *Dictionary of the Old Testament: Historical Books*. After examining every reference about women in these books in the Old Testament, she admits that the Pentateuch's world is "patriarchal" and that the culture of Israel was a "strongly masculine-dominated one."

Catherine Clark Kroeger, another evangelical, wrote the article on "Women" for the same publisher's *Dictionary of New Testament Background*, where she opens up with this statement: "In the main, history is written by, for and about men."[3] Our Bible is like this. We can pretend it is not, but pretending leads us to an ironic commitment to our faith and into hidden secrets and despair. Why not, I sometimes ask myself, just admit it? Will the Bible lose its power? By no means.

Does the Bible at times transcend that masculine-shaped story? Indeed it does, and it often does, and for that we can be profoundly grateful. But it is dishonest for us to say anything less. Our Bible is shaped by a male perspective because God, in his wisdom, chose to speak in those days in those ways. Our God is a living God; our God spoke within history and shaped that history to move us into the world in which we now live. I think we need to be careful about how we say this sort of thing, but that carefulness also means admitting that (primarily, if not solely) male authors wrote the Bible's books.

In General

One of the most knowledgeable scholars about women and the ancient world is David Scholer. In a dictionary article in the same series of dictionaries mentioned above on women in the ministry of Jesus, David writes this: "In very general terms Jesus lived in social-cultural contexts (the Jewish context and the larger Greco-Roman society) in which the male view of women was usually negative and the place of women was understood to be limited for the most part to the domestic roles of wife and mother."[4] Here is a famous statement made by the Jewish historian Josephus, a contemporary of Jesus and the apostle Paul: "The woman," Josephus informs his audience, "says the Law, is in all things inferior to the man."[5]

In general, then, women were perceived as inferior. But there were plenty of exceptions, exceptions that reveal an undercurrent that would eventually alter the current itself. Let's look at one woman in that undercurrent. A wonderful fictional story of liberation is told of a Jewish woman named Judith in the Old Testament Apocrypha. The story transcends even the drama of the stories of Deborah and Esther, two Old Testament women—one a judge and the other a beautiful, wise, and clever woman. Judith uses her rhetorical and sexual charms to deliver Israel from the Assyrians by intrigue, and then she decapitates the king with his own sword and carries off his head in her kosher bag! No one suggests we should follow her example, but it is not without some significance that we find here some female heroes in the Jewish world.

Again, in general women were seen as inferior to men. The church, for any number of reasons, fossilized this tradition into a rigid distinction between men and women when it came to ministries in the church. A good example of this teaching can be found in Augustine, one of the most powerful theologians in the history of the church.[6] Augustine thought women were companions for men in the sense that they were designed to be procreative partners. Furthermore, though he believed women were human, he did not believe women *are* God's image. Males are the image of God. A woman "bears" God's image but a man "is" God's image. By marriage, Augustine taught, a woman can become the image of God. What should be noted is that culture itself gave rise to this view of women and there was little incentive for Augustine to challenge it. I have no desire to trash Augustine; we are deeply indebted to much good in his theology. But the culture surrounding him and the kind of theology that found its way in that culture devastated some passages in the Bible.

Please understand that I am not saying the church had a uniformly negative view of women; it didn't.[7] More importantly, the widespread restriction of women from teaching and preaching ministries damaged the church's witness, because for centuries this became the tradition *through* which the church read its Bible. More could be said, and more deserves to be said, but this is not a book on the history of women in the church.[8] I use this example merely to illustrate the general view taken by the majority of the church. There were exceptions, of course. The exceptions, however, were just that.

What Should We Do?

The question we need to ask today is this, and this question strikes to the heart of how we read the Bible: Do we seek to retrieve that cultural world and those cultural expressions, or do we live the same gospel in a different way in a different day? Is this a return and retrieve it all, a return and retrieve some, a reading of the Bible *through* tradition, or a reading of the Bible *with* tradition? Or, and I think this is the case, is this a tradition that needs to be challenged?

We could probably sketch out a dozen or so views of how Christians approach what the Bible says about women in church ministries, but many today are willing to eyeball it into three basic options.[9] Two views are connected to what might be called the tradition (hard patriarchy and soft patriarchy), while one is more connected to a renew-and-renewing mindset: mutuality (sometimes called evangelical egalitarianism).[10]

The *hard patriarchy* view believes the biblical context and its teachings are more or less both God's original and permanent design. A woman's responsibility is to glorify God, to love God, to love others, and to love her husband and her children. That is, if she is married and has children (exceptions duly noted). More narrowly now, she must submit to her husband in all things, she must submit to male leadership in the church in all things, and she should also not find her way into leadership in society. For whatever reason, God ordained males to be leaders. The hard patriarchy view shapes life by a perception of the divine order in gender and roles; it believes these roles will create peace. "God's purpose in ordering marriage is peace. One takes the husband's role, one takes the wife's role, one in guiding, one in supporting. If both had the very same roles, there would be no peace."[11]

The *soft patriarchy* view believes the biblical context is cultural but the principles are permanent. We are called to find a living analogy in our Western, twenty-first-century context to the teachings of the Bible, including the teaching of gender roles. A woman's responsibility is to glorify God, to love God, to love others, and — if married — to love her husband and her children (if there are any). More narrowly now, while affirming the importance of submission and gender and roles, this view frees the woman to do more than the hard patriarchy view. She can work outside the home in any manner for which she is qualified and competent, always with her primary role being wife and mother. She can participate in an appropriate female manner at church, but this would not include being senior pastor or teaching or leading men in any way.

I believe that both of the above views, to one degree or another, are stuck in the fall of humankind. We must remind ourselves over and over again that the Bible's story is a story from:

> God's Trinitarian oneness, to
> the Adam, who was one and alone, to
> Adam and Eve, who were one and together, to
> Adam and Eve and others, who through sin become others, to
> Jesus Christ, who was the one God incarnate, to
> becoming one (as in Eden) all over again in Christ, to
> the consummation, when we will be one with God and others.

Whatever we say about women in church ministries, about women in marriages, or about women who are single must be connected to this story. I believe the next view makes the most sense of how women fit into the Bible's story.

The *mutuality* view, which taps into this "oneness-otherness-oneness" theme deeply, also believes a woman's responsibility is to glorify God, to love God, to love others, and — again if married and if with children — to love her husband and her children. More narrowly, a mutuality view liberates women from the tradition because it believes the biblical context is cultural and that even the biblical teachings reflect that culture. Even more importantly, it knows that reading the Bible *through* a long-established church tradition needs to be challenged.

Instead of seeking to impose that culture and those culturally shaped teachings on women in a completely different world and culture, the mutuality view summons Christians to the Bible one more time. It knows the story of the Bible is one in which Jesus Christ makes men and women one again, in Christ and in marriage. And, in conscious dependence on the Spirit in the context of a community of faith that seeks to live out that oneness, it gives to women the freedom to discern what God has called them to do — whatever it might be, including preaching, teaching, and leading in the church. The conclusions are that women are encouraged by the "exceptions" of the Bible — and there are more than most realize — and by passages like the mutuality or equality principle in Galatians 3:28, to explore God's gifts to women. Moreover, the ongoing guidance of the Spirit may lead women into ministries that break down the tradition.

Jesus told us the Spirit would guide us, and this book is an attempt to sketch how that guidance works itself out for many of us. Here are Jesus' words, which I will quote before we look at the biblical exceptions that provide a map for our guidance: "But when he, the Spirit of truth, comes, he will guide you into all the truth. He will not speak on his own; he will speak only what he hears, and he will tell you what is yet to come" (John 16:13).

Do we believe this? I do. Do you? To believe this verse we must have the confidence to strike out in conscious dependence on the Spirit.

We do so not by charting our own path through the thicket but by mastering the plot and the story of the Bible so that the path we take is the natural, Spirit-led waterslide that will guide us to the waters in our world in our way. Let me expand now our image of the waterslide. For many, the tradition about women in church ministries is not just a bank on the side of the slide but a bank that is growing and expanding and restricting the movement of the slider on her way down the slide. The intent of the next two chapters is to put the tradition in its (biblical) place.

Chapter 12

What Did Women Do in the Old Testament?

Women in Church Ministries 2

Many of my friends, when a discussion arises about women in church ministries, gravitate to Paul's two famous statements — that women should be silent in the churches:

> Women should remain *silent* in the churches. They are *not allowed to speak*, but must be in submission, as the law says. If they want to inquire about something, they should ask their own husbands at home; for it is disgraceful for a woman to speak in the church. (1 Corinthians 14:34 – 35, emphasis added)

> A woman should learn *in quietness and full submission*. I do not permit a woman to teach or to assume authority over a man; *she must be quiet.* (1 Timothy 2:11 – 12, emphasis added)

Some of my friends are for and some are against women in leadership ministries. Both kinds of friends gravitate to these texts. For me, it's like asking about marriage in the Bible and gravitating toward the divorce texts. Yes, I say, these statements by Paul about silence are important and we will look at them in due time, but there is something else we should do first.

Know the Story of the Bible

The story of the Bible tells us stories about women that I call stories of "WDWD." Many of you know about the bracelet that some have worn since the mid-1990s with these letters on it: WWJD. Those letters stand for "What Would Jesus Do?" and they are a moral reminder of our renew-and-renewing approach to the Bible to live as Jesus would have us live in our day and in our way. My WDWD acronym is one we should consider when we think about women in church ministries: What Did Women Do? in Bible times. In one of my classes at North Park I ask students to chart what many of the women in the Bible did, and as the class progresses, the charts get longer and the activities of women more obvious. You might try it on your own.

To name some of the more obvious women, think of Miriam, Deborah, and Huldah; think of Esther and the woman in the Song of Songs; think of Priscilla, Junia, and Phoebe. Think (and this is hard to do for Protestants) of Mary, mother of Jesus, whose influence on Jesus, James, and some early Christians is largely ignored. Many more names could be invoked but need not quite yet. Our point is what *these women* did.

What did they do? They led, they prophesied, they taught, they were apostles, and they were local church mentors. At this point, all we need to grant is that there are—at a minimum—women who were *exceptions* to dominant cultural perception of women as inferior. They were exceptions whom God raised above the norm in order to accomplish his will. I will go beyond the word "exception" in what follows, but for now we can ask if we are permitting women exceptions in our churches. I know many who believe there should be no exceptions—and they are caging and silencing even the exceptional blue parakeet.

In my conversations with friends after we have discussed both the WDWD passages and the "Women Keep Silence Passages" (WKSP), I always conclude with this question: Do you permit women to do in your churches what women did in the Bible and in the early churches?

No matter how seriously you take the WKSPs, it is profoundly unbibli-

cal to let those passages overcome the WDWDs so that all we have left is silenced and caged blue parakeets! Whatever Paul meant by silence, he did not mean to say that the WDWD passages were now obsolete. The silence, in fact, is biblical only if it permits women to do today what women can be found doing in the WDWDs!

So now we ask: What did women do in the Bible?[1] If we want to be biblical, this question needs to be asked and answered. Until it is, we will not be biblical. I believe reading the Bible *through* tradition has prevented us even from asking the question, let alone answering it. The place to begin is with an all-encompassing text — the creation narrative — that establishes how the Bible's story is to be read.

Creation and New Creation

If we read the Bible as Story, we begin all questions of the Bible at the beginning, with Genesis 1 – 3. And if we begin here, the entire story is reshaped. We learn from these chapters that *God created male and female as mutuals — made for each other — and they were at one with each another.* The fall distorted mutuality by turning women against men and men against women; oneness became otherness and rivalry for power. Here are the climactic, tragic words from Genesis 3:16: "Your desire will be for your husband, and he will rule over you."

The fall turned the woman to seek dominance over the man, and the fall turned the man to seek dominance over the woman. A life of struggling for control is the way of life for the fallen. But the good news story of the Bible is that the fall eventually gives way to new creation; the fallen can be reborn and re-created. Sadly, the church has far too often *perpetuated the fall as a permanent condition.* Perpetuating the fall entails failing to *restore creation conditions* when it comes to male and female relationships. This is against both Jesus and Paul, who each read the Bible as a story that moves from creation (oneness) to new creation (oneness).

Jesus informed his disciples that although Moses permitted divorce, which annihilates the Creator's designed union in marriage, divorce was *not God's original intention.* Permanence, love, oneness, and mutuality were God's intent in original creation. Jesus, then, appeals to Story, to the original creation, to show how God's people are supposed to live in the new creation. Moses' permission for divorce pertains, so it seems to me, to a life too deeply marred by the fall. A Jesus community undoes the distortions of the fall because it seeks to live out the fullness of the Story.

The apostle Paul twice appeals to original creation to explain God's redemption. In 2 Corinthians 5:17 Paul says: "If anyone is in Christ, *the new creation* has come: The old [the fall] has gone, the new [creation] is here!" (emphasis added). What can this mean but that the implications of the fall are being undone for those who are in Christ? This draws us directly back to Genesis 3:16 to see that the otherness struggle between the sexes for control has been ended because we are now in the new creation. New creation means we are being restored to the equality and mutuality of Genesis 1–2.

Paul does much the same in Galatians 3:28: "There is neither Jew nor Gentile, neither slave nor free, *neither male nor female*, for you are all *one* in Christ Jesus" (emphasis added). The words Paul uses for "male ... female" are quoted from Genesis 1:27, the original creation story. The word "one" evokes God's oneness and God's design for oneness among his created beings. What is Paul claiming here? He is—and notice this carefully—contending that in Christ we return to Eden's mutuality. He is contending that life in Christ creates unity, equality, and oneness.

What we learn from Genesis 1–2, then, is that God originally made Adam and Eve as mutuals, that the fall distorted that relationship, and that the story of the Bible's plot leads us to see redemption in Christ as new creation. Both Jesus and Paul see in Genesis 1–2 the original design for what Christ's redemption brings to men and women in this world. If there is any place in the world where this mutuality should be restored, it should be in the church. Ironically, it can be the least redemptive place of the week!

We now move to some specific women in the Old Testament. That these three women are not household names concerns me, not just because it means that we don't read our Bibles thoroughly enough. No, what concerns me more is that we can discuss women in church ministries without taking into consideration concrete examples of what women did in the Bible. The principle of WDWD brings them to the table.

Miriam, Deborah, and Huldah

That God could raise up into leadership women who exercised considerable authority can be seen in three women who come alive in the pages of the Old Testament. They are part of Israel's story, and no storytelling is fair that does not include them. Miriam was one of Israel's spiritual leaders, Deborah was a presidential leader of God's people, and Huldah was a prophet above (mostly male) prophets.

Miriam: Spiritual Leader

Miriam was one-third of Israel's triumvirate of leadership: Moses as lawgiver, Aaron as priest, and Miriam as prophetess. When the children of Israel escaped the clutches of Pharaoh, it was Miriam who led the Israelites into worship with these inspired words:

> *Sing to the LORD,*
> *for he is highly exalted.*
> *Both horse and driver*
> *he has hurled into the sea. (Exodus 15:21)*

The Song of Moses, found now at Exodus 15:1 – 18, may well have been composed under inspiration by Miriam. Other women are found singing within the pages of the Bible's story—women like Deborah (Judges 5:1 – 31), Hannah (1 Samuel 2:1 – 10), and Mary (Luke 1:46 – 55). Singing was connected to the gift of prophecy in the Bible (1 Chronicles 25:1 – 8). When a later prophet, Micah, spoke of Israel's deliverance, he saw three leaders in Israel: "I brought you up out of Egypt ... I sent Moses to lead you, also Aaron and Miriam" (Micah 6:4).

Miriam was the one who fetched Moses from the Nile; as Moses' older sister she no doubt participated in Moses' own family celebrations of Passover in Egypt; and as older sister she sang alongside Moses and Aaron about God's deliverance. In Numbers 12 she sticks her neck out: Miriam thought Moses' choice of wife inappropriate and summarily gives him the business and gossips with Aaron about him (Numbers 12:1). God summons them both, but clearly Miriam is the problem here for she is envious of Moses' expanding power and jealous of her own reputation. "Hasn't he [the LORD] also spoken through us?" she asks, knowing full well the answer (yes) and the silliness of her stance. The Lord reveals to both Miriam and Aaron that prophets (as she is) hear from God in dreams and visions, but God speaks with Moses "face-to-face." God is not happy with Aaron and Miriam and departs, and when the cloud of glory settles Miriam has a defiling skin disease on her hands. Aaron calls for a family prayer meeting in which Moses petitions God and Miriam is healed.

It takes some *chutzpah* to speak against Moses, and we should not condone what Miriam (or Aaron) did. But what we should see is the strength, power, and authority Miriam possessed that led her to think that she, even she, could call Moses into question. She made a mistake, a serious one, but it was not because she was a woman. It was because she envied Moses — her sin was envy, not being a woman. Her sin was no different from that of other leaders in the Old Testament, including Moses (who does not get to enter the Promised Land) or David (whose sins sprinkled the kingdom). Miriam was a blue parakeet who was permitted to sing because God had given her his voice.

Deborah: Presidential Leader

Deborah was, to use modern analogies, the president, the pope, and Rambo all bundled up in one female body! Judges 4–5 reveals that God called women — it is not mentioned that she is an "exception" — to lead his people. Every reading of her story reveals she was exceptional.

Like Miriam, Deborah was a *prophet*: "Now Deborah, a prophet, the wife of Lappidoth, was leading [*shapat*] Israel at that time" (Judges 4:4). When the Bible says she was "leading" Israel, it uses the term for the *judge* of Israel. She was to her generation what Moses was to his. The word translated "judged" (*shapat*) combines the ideas of "national leadership," "judicial decisions," and "political, military savior." If we ask what did women do, and we ask this question of Deborah, we learn that women could speak for God as a prophet, render decisions in a law court as a judge, exercise leadership over the entire spiritual-social Israel, and be a military commander who brought Israel to victory. To use other terms, she led the nation spiritually, musically, legally, politically, and militarily. Let us not pretend her tasks were social and secular; Deborah was a woman leader of the entire people of God.

Deborah's theology flows gloriously out of the Song of Deborah in Judges 5. I include her words here and ask you to read this song, saying it aloud, and then jot down some ideas about her theology. I will offer minimal commentary as we read this text together. Barak, under the leadership of Deborah, defeated Jabin, king of Canaan, and they sang together this masterpiece victory song, which clearly is Deborah's Spirit-led own song:

On that day Deborah and Barak son of Abinoam sang this song:

> *"When the princes in Israel take the lead,*
> *when the people willingly offer themselves —*
> *praise the LORD!*
>
> *"Hear this, you kings! Listen, you rulers!*
> *I, even I, will sing to the LORD;*
> *I will praise the LORD, the God of Israel, in song.*

[Notice that God's victory over the Canaanites reaches back into the victory of God through the Exodus, the giving of the Torah, the forming of the covenant, and entry into the land:]

> *"When you, LORD, went out from Seir,*
> *when you marched from the land of Edom,*

the earth shook, the heavens poured,
  the clouds poured down water.

The mountains quaked before the LORD, the One of Sinai,
  before the LORD, the God of Israel.

[Israel began to fade in its commitment until Deborah, "a mother in Israel," arose to stir the nation to action:]

"In the days of Shamgar son of Anath,
  in the days of Jael, the highways were abandoned;
    travelers took to winding paths.

Villagers in Israel would not fight;
  they held back until I, Deborah, arose,
    until I arose, a mother in Israel.

God chose new leaders
  when war came to the city gates,
but not a shield or spear was seen
  among forty thousand in Israel.

[Those who mustered the courage to act in good faith are now praised by Deborah:]

My heart is with Israel's princes,
  with the willing volunteers among the people.
    Praise the LORD!

"You who ride on white donkeys,
  sitting on your saddle blankets,
    and you who walk along the road,
consider the voice of the singers at the watering places.
  They recite the victories of the LORD,
    the victories of his villagers in Israel.
"Then the people of the LORD
  went down to the city gates.

'Wake up, wake up, Deborah!
  Wake up, wake up, break out in song!

Arise, Barak!
Take captive your captives, son of Abinoam.'

[The roll call of participants in the battle:]

"The remnant of the nobles came down;
the people of the LORD came down to me against the mighty.

Some came from Ephraim, whose roots were in Amalek;
Benjamin was with the people who followed you.
From Makir captains came down,
from Zebulun those who bear a commander's staff.

The princes of Issachar were with Deborah;
yes, Issachar was with Barak,
sent under his command into the valley.
In the districts of Reuben
there was much searching of heart.

Why did you stay among the sheep pens
to hear the whistling for the flocks?
In the districts of Reuben
there was much searching of heart.

Gilead stayed beyond the Jordan.
And Dan, why did he linger by the ships?
Asher remained on the coast
and stayed in his coves.

The people of Zebulun risked their very lives;
so did Naphtali on the terraced fields.

[The battle is fought against Canaan and its leader, Sisera. God's people win, and Deborah's triumph becomes clear as she sums up what was recounted one chapter earlier in Judges:]

"Kings came, they fought,
the kings of Canaan fought.
At Taanach, by the waters of Megiddo,
they took no plunder of silver.

From the heavens the stars fought,
from their courses they fought against Sisera.

The river Kishon swept them away,
the age-old river, the river Kishon.
March on, my soul; be strong!
Then thundered the horses' hooves—
galloping, galloping go his mighty steeds.

[Meroz, a village that acts faithlessly, is cursed by Deborah because they are not loyal to God:]

'Curse Meroz,' said the angel of the LORD.
'Curse its people bitterly,
because they did not come to help the LORD,
to help the LORD against the mighty.'

[Barak, because he sought help, did not finish off the victory; instead, Jael, a woman, kills Sisera. Yes, of course, the battle is gruesome and the victory bloody and the language graphic:]

"Most blessed of women be Jael,
the wife of Heber the Kenite,
most blessed of tent-dwelling women.

He asked for water, and she gave him milk;
in a bowl fit for nobles she brought him curdled milk.

Her hand reached for the tent peg,
her right hand for the laborer's hammer.
She struck Sisera, she crushed his head,
she shattered and pierced his temple.

At her feet he sank,
he fell; there he lay.
At her feet he sank, he fell;
where he sank, there he fell—dead.

[Deborah turns to recount the experience of military victory through the eyes of another woman, the mother of Sisera, the fallen Canaanite king, who thinks the delay of her son is because he's mopping up Israel. Deborah has the last word, and it strikes the modern reader as a combination of bitter contempt and exultant satire:]

> *"Through the window peered Sisera's mother;*
> *behind the lattice she cried out,*
> *'Why is his chariot so long in coming?*
> *Why is the clatter of his chariots delayed?'*
>
> *The wisest of her ladies answer her;*
> *indeed, she keeps saying to herself,*
>
> *'Are they not finding and dividing the spoils:*
> *a woman or two for each man,*
> *colorful garments as plunder for Sisera,*

[I interrupt; the singer and reader know that Sisera's mother, who is depicted as staring through the lattice in anticipation of victory, is living a dream. The reality is that the "highly embroidered garments for my neck" she is about to mention turned out to be sackcloth and ashes.]

> *colorful garments embroidered,*
> *highly embroidered garments for my neck —*
> *all this as plunder?'*

[In a final flourish Deborah seeks the glory of God for those who love God and sure defeat for those who do not:]

> *"So may all your enemies perish, LORD!*
> *But may all who love you be like the sun*
> *when it rises in its strength."*

Then the land had peace forty years.

The courage of this woman is remarkable. Her theology is bathed in zeal for the Lord, her exhortations capable of drawing all to the battle plain, and her hopes inspiring to this day. I shudder at her *Schadenfreude*, her "joy over the defeat of her enemies," but I trust our zeal for God's glory is as resolute as hers. If there is any single line that captures the spiritual vision of Deborah it is verse 21c: "March on, my soul; be strong!" This, too, is part of our story.

Deborah is a blue parakeet who was permitted to sing and fly.

Huldah: Prophet above the Prophets

When King Josiah is informed of the discovery of the long-lost Torah in the temple, a certain Shaphan reads the text to Josiah. The king, who has "the most responsive royal heart since the hearing heart of Solomon,"[2] realizes the nation has failed to live according to God's covenant. He falls apart in godly repentance and needs discernment. What should he do? To which of God's prophets shall he send word to consult? Here are his options: he can consult Jeremiah, Zephaniah, Nahum, Habakkuk, or Huldah. The first four have books in Israel's collection of prophets. But he chooses the female prophet, Huldah, above the rest. Huldah is not chosen because no men were available; she is chosen because she is truly exceptional among the prophets.

She confirms that the scroll is indeed God's Torah and this, in some sense, authorizes this text as Israel's Scriptures from this time on. Furthermore, prophetess Huldah, unafraid to tell the truth, informs Josiah that indeed God's wrath is against the disobedience of this nation. But, she adds, because the king has humbled himself before God, he will be gathered to his ancestors in peace. All of this is found in 2 Kings 22.

Huldah is a female blue parakeet who sang among a company of males.

Conclusion

From this brief sketch, we can repeat the question: What did women do?

> They spoke for God;
> they led the nation in every department;
> they sanctioned Scripture; and
> they guided nations back to the path of righteousness.

These women were blue parakeets who were allowed to fly and to sing.

But that was then, and this is now. What about in the New Testament? Did women's roles decrease or increase? If one takes into consideration the story form of the Bible and one considers that Jesus ushers in the beginning of new creation, one should not be surprised to learn that women begin where the Old Testament leaves off and take on newer responsibilities. That is exactly what happens.

Chapter 13

What Did Women Do in the New Testament?

Women in Church Ministries 3

A young woman came to me at the end of class and said, "I'm so upset." I asked her why. "Because I've never heard about any of these women we have been studying."

"Which women?" you might ask. Junia, Priscilla, and Phoebe.

Let me ask you (the reader) a question: Do you know about these women? If your experience is like this student's, you have every right to ask why or why not. My experience is that more don't know these women than do.

You are also entitled to ask why so many Protestants totally ignore the most significant woman in the entire Bible, Mary, mother of Jesus. We begin with her and we ask again, WDWD? (in the New Testament). As we ask this question of Mary and other New Testament women, the entire theme of oneness—of God's restoring men and women to be one in Christ—begins to take on concrete realities.

MARY: A Woman of Influence

Mary makes some Protestants break out in an emotional rash and rant; I've seen it happen. Once when I told an older woman that I was studying what the Bible says about Mary, she said to me, "Why? She's so Catholic!" Ah, I thought, that's reading the Bible *through* the (anti-Catholic) tradition! We believe in the Bible, and it reveals that Mary was a woman of influence, and some of that influence, if you weigh the verses carefully, had to be at the level of teaching.

To begin with, Mary was the mother of the Messiah, and it was no small vocation to be part of forming Jesus the Messiah as he matured. Furthermore, if the early tradition is accurate, Mary was a widow, so when we look at her influence in the early church, we are looking at a widow. I see her influence in the New Testament in three ways. Mary's influence emerges in her training of Jesus and of his brother James, and she was critical in the formation of our Gospels.

Mary had a powerful influence on her sons — including Jesus. Themes from Mary's majestic Magnificat show up so centrally both in the teachings of Jesus and in the letter of James, I believe it is clear that Mary *taught* and was involved in the *spiritual formation* of Jesus and James.[1] I would not want to claim that Jesus learned only from Mary; of course he learned from Joseph and from others. But can we expect that God would give Mary to Jesus as a mother and not qualify her to be a singular and godly influence on him? I think not.

Perhaps turning to another of Mary's sons, James, is a safer way to make this point. Here are the words of Mary's Spirit-prompted Magnificat (Luke 1:46–55):

And Mary said:

> *"My soul glorifies the Lord*
> *and my spirit rejoices in God my Savior,*
> *for he has been mindful*
> *of the humble state of his servant.*
> *From now on all generations will call me blessed,*
> *for the Mighty One has done great things for me —*
> *holy is his name.*

His mercy extends to those who fear him,
    from generation to generation.
He has performed mighty deeds with his arm;
    he has scattered those who are proud in their inmost thoughts.
He has brought down rulers from their thrones
    but has lifted up the humble.
He has filled the hungry with good things
    but has sent the rich away empty.
He has helped his servant Israel,
    remembering to be merciful
to Abraham and his descendants forever,
    just as he promised our ancestors."

The themes of Mary's song are clear: justice for the poor and marginalized, judgment on the oppressors, holiness, and God's faithfulness to his covenant promises. James opens up his letter with these words:

> Believers in humble circumstances [or the "poor"] ought to take pride in their high position. But the rich should take pride in their humiliation — since they will pass away like a wild flower. For the sun rises with scorching heat and withers the plant; its blossom falls and its beauty is destroyed. In the same way, the rich will fade away even while they go about their business. (James 1:9–11)

This prediction of a reversal of fortunes is a central theme to the Magnificat and a central theme in Jesus' own teachings. It punctuates nearly every chapter of James's book.

But what strikes me when I read James are these words from James 1:27: "Religion that God our Father accepts as pure and faultless is this: to look after orphans and widows in their distress and to keep oneself from being polluted by the world." James and Jesus and their other brothers and sisters were, in terms of first-century Jews, "orphans" because they did not have a living father. An orphan in that society was anyone who had lost one of his or her parents. Furthermore, James states that showing compassion for orphans and widows—like his mother—reveals the presence of genuine "religion" or "piety."

I cannot prove that either James or Jesus got these ideas from their mother. But what we ought to consider is that the Spirit-inspired woman who was their mother, the one who uttered potent warnings about the rich oppressors and made wonderfully comforting promises to the oppressed poor, rocked their cradles, taught them to sing, and explained to them their "family history" (how does one explain the plan of God to bring the Messiah when one is the mother of the Messiah?) had a nurturing impact on the boys that unquestionably shows up in what they believe, how they act, and what they teach. It doesn't matter that she is a woman. What matters are her godliness, her compassion, her intelligence, and her devotion.

One more point makes sense to me and I hope to you. Where did you think Luke acquired the stories he tells us in Luke 1–2? There are only a few possible sources: God, Mary, Joseph, Zechariah, Elizabeth, Simeon, Anna, Jesus, and his brothers and sisters. The only person who knew the story of Mary's words with the angel Gabriel was Mary; Luke may have not spoken with Mary (though I think Luke easily could have since he was in and around Jerusalem collecting information for his gospel), but somehow what he learned about those early days of impregnation and song somehow came from Mary. However you look at it, *the first two chapters of our gospel of Luke derive somehow from Mary.*

What did women do? Mary *influenced* her messianic Son, her New Testament-writing son James,[2] and *provided information* to Luke as seeds for stories that got his gospel off to a great start.

JUNIA: An Apostle above Other Apostles

Do you know who Junia is? Here's all we know: "Greet Andronicus and *Junia*, my fellow Jews who have been in prison with me. They are *outstanding among the apostles*, and they were in Christ before I was" (Romans 16:7, emphasis added). Here are words of utter profundity, words that have been silenced like a blue parakeet perhaps more than any other words in the Bible about women: "outstanding among the apostles." Junia is an outstanding (woman) apostle, though to be sure, being a woman had little to do with it. What mattered were her intelligence, her giftedness, and her calling.

Junia is a woman's name. But because women aren't supposed to be "apostles," someone copying the letter to the Romans changed the spelling so that Junia (female) became Junias (male). The RSV of 1946 has "Andronicus and Junias" and adds "men of note among the apostles." Recent exhaustive study has uncovered this mistake, and we now are virtually certain "Junia" was a female.[3] And she was an "apostle"! Junia and her husband-apostle Andronicus were relatives of Paul, they came to faith in Christ prior to Paul's own conversion, and they were imprisoned with Paul (no doubt because they were believers and leaders among the Christians).

But more importantly, Andronicus and Junia are "outstanding" or "prominent" (NRSV) among apostles. This could mean they were recognized as leaders *by* the apostles, but the evidence in the early church is that everyone translated this expression as "prominent apostles" among the first generation of Christians. Perhaps we should take a deep breath and get our bearings before we go any further. A statement by St. Chrysostom, a famous preacher and theologian who read and preached in Greek, seals the deal; I put in italics the most significant words:

> "Greet Andronicus and Junia ... who are outstanding among the apostles": *To be an apostle* is something great. *But to be outstanding among the apostles*—just think what a wonderful song of praise that is! They were outstanding on the basis of their works and virtuous actions. *Indeed, how great the wisdom of this woman must have been that she was even deemed worthy of the title of apostle.*

We draw two conclusions: Junia was a woman and Junia was an apostle.

But what kind of apostle? Some forget to ask and answer this question. She clearly was not one of the twelve apostles chosen and sent out by Jesus. So, what kind was she? The answer is in the Bible. As the story of the Bible unfolds, not only were there the twelve apostles but there were some "lesser" apostles — what Wheaton Professor Doug Moo calls "traveling missionaries."[4] There were others in the New Testament called "apostle" in this sense, including Barnabas (Acts 14:14), James (Galatians 1:19), Epaphroditus (Philippians 2:25), and those who are called "apostles of the churches" (2 Corinthians 8:23). Even if we rank Junia among the missionary apostles, she is still an apostle and is considered top drawer for her work.

What kind of work did that involve? Otherwise stated, what did women do? We cannot be sure but probably these kinds of things: Junia, along with her husband, Andronicus, were commissioned or recognized as having gifts from God. Those gifts involved such things as evangelizing, teaching, preaching, establishing, and leading churches. Underneath it all would have been an exemplary character of godliness and love that provided a template for others to observe and imitate.

PRISCILLA: A Teacher of Scripture and Theology

We know much more about Priscilla, the wife of Aquila, than we do of Junia. Aquila and Priscilla were from Rome (Acts 18:2); they were kicked out of Rome when Claudius ordered all "Jews" to evacuate. They became acquainted with Paul in Corinth and began to make tents together (18:3). This friendship led to their traveling with Paul to Ephesus, where — and here we are offered another glimpse into what women did in the early churches — Priscilla and Aquila "explained to [Apollos] the way of God more adequately" (18:26). This husband and wife, instead of fighting for power with one another (cf. Genesis 3:16), worked together for the gospel. The mutuality theme is obvious here.

There are some details here that deserve a careful look. First, Priscilla's name is almost always given first. Listing a woman's name first was not impossible in the ancient world, but it was unusual. More significantly, she is almost always named before her husband, leading many to think she was the leading light when it came to this ministry. Notice these references: Acts 18:18, 19, 26; Romans 16:3; 2 Timothy 4:19. The only exceptions are Acts 18:2 and 1 Corinthians 16:19. We should not make too much of her name being first since she may have had more social status in the Roman world.

More importantly, "they"—and again her name is first—"explained" to the scholar Apollos "the way of God more adequately." Priscilla knew her theology and her Bible, and she knew it so well she could lead Apollos from a John-the-Baptist faith to a Jesus-faith. This husband-wife team taught Apollos so well he was able—two verses later—to refute nonmessianic Jews in public debate by opening up the Scriptures for them (Acts 18:28). Clearly Priscilla was a theological teacher. This is why Priscilla and Aquila are called Paul's "co-workers" in Romans 16:3.[5] "Co-worker" was Paul's special term for his associates *in church ministries*. What did they do? They—including Priscilla—shared with Paul in being called by God, in preaching the gospel, in carrying on pastoral work with churches, and in risking their lives for their faith.

So what did women do in the New Testament church? We have one woman who was an apostle and another one who was a fellow worker and teacher. We must look at one more—a woman who was at a minimum the official interpreter of Paul's letter to the Romans!

PHOEBE: Deacon and Benefactor

I commend to you our sister Phoebe, a *deacon* of the church in Cenchreae. I ask you to receive her in the Lord in a way worthy of his people and to give her any help she may need from you, for she has been the *benefactor* of many people, including me. (Romans 16:1–2, emphasis added)

One of the most noticeable features of women in the earliest churches was that they directed their own households. So, when the churches moved into the homes, these household-directing women became de facto directors and leaders of local household churches. A good example is Phoebe. Unlike Priscilla and Junia, who were both married, Phoebe's husband is not mentioned. This could indicate that she was single. Perhaps she was a widow. We cannot be sure. She stands in this text alone as a single woman. What matters is her calling from God and her giftedness. Paul tells us that she was from Cenchreae, a city just outside of Corinth in Greece, and that she had traveled to Rome. What did Phoebe do?

To begin with, Phoebe is called a "deacon." This word "deacon" is the same word in the New Testament, whether the person is a man or a woman, for a leader in the church. When Paul calls her "deacon," he is not thinking of the "deaconesses" in our churches who clean up communion cups in the church kitchen. Phoebe is called "deacon" because she exercised a ministry, or service, in the church.

What kind of ministry? Deacons are often connected to "ministry/service of the word" in Paul's letters — see, for example, 1 Corinthians 3:5 – 9.[6] But, since Phoebe is called "a deacon *of the church* in Cenchreae," we should think of her "ministry" in terms of the list of qualifications and ministries we find in 1 Timothy 3:8 – 12. Doug Moo describes a safe conclusion: "It is likely that deacons were charged with visitation of the sick, poor relief, and perhaps financial oversight."[7] Others think more is involved, that is, that "deacon" describes an official ministry of God's Word. I think the latter view may be closer to the facts, though it is unwise to stretch the evidence to fit what we'd like to be true.

At some level Phoebe was a "minister." She was also significant. When Paul asks the church at Rome to "receive her," he surely has in mind that they are to roll out a red carpet of hospitality — the way they do for "saints." But it is also possible that Phoebe, a benefactor or wealthy patron of Paul's ministry of bringing the gospel to the Roman Empire, was responsible for getting this letter to the right people. Most today think Phoebe was Paul's courier for the letter to the Romans. Since couriers were charged with responsibility to explain their letters,

Phoebe probably read the letter aloud and answered questions the Roman Christians may have had. (If today's Christians, who struggle to make sense of this dense treatise called Romans, are any indication, then Phoebe may have spent days explaining this letter to the Roman churches.) Phoebe, to put this graphically, can be seen as the first "commentator" on the letter to the Romans.[8]

One more point. A recent exhaustive commentary on Romans by Robert Jewett contends that Phoebe is not just a "benefactor" in an ordinary sense but that she is the patron for Paul's strategic plan to preach the gospel from Rome to Spain.[9] We cannot be sure that Phoebe's role is that defined, but there are enough hints here to suggest that Phoebe was an important part of Paul's letter to the Romans as well as his missionary strategy. One of her most important contributions was providing funds. It is worth noting that in the fourth century, in an inscription found on Jerusalem's Mount of Olives, a woman named Sophia was called the "new Phoebe" or the "second Phoebe" because of her financial support for Christian ministries.[10]

What Did Women Do?

What did women do? Another way of asking this question is this: What did women do if we read the New Testament as Story? How do we see the oneness theme begin to take shape in the story of the New Testament?

Mary was influential with Jesus and James and gave to Luke crucial information for writing his gospel. *Junia* was an apostle who was involved in missionary work. *Priscilla* taught Bible and theology alongside her husband. *Phoebe* financially supported the apostle Paul in his ministry, carried the letter to Rome, and helped to explain its contents as Paul prepared for his Spanish mission. WDWD? They were influential, they were a source for stories about Jesus, they were church planters, they were teachers, they were benefactors and interpreters of Paul's letters.

Furthermore, we learn a little more about each: Junia and Priscilla were married, but Mary was a widow and Phoebe may well have been single. There is no indication that women could teach and lead only if they were connected to a male who was also a leader. And, to tie these four women into the story of the Bible, each of these women exhibits the mutuality (or oneness) theme that begins in creation, is threatened by the fall, and begins to become more and more a reality in Christ.

If women did all this, why does Paul speak of silencing women in public assemblies? How does such silencing fit within the theme of oneness — of God's work of redemption, restoring men and women into unity in Christ? This is where reading the Bible as Story, asking WDWD?, becomes important. Furthermore, it means that though we may read the Bible *with* tradition (where women are silenced), we are at times called to challenge the tradition, which we will do in the next chapter.

Chapter 14

Silencing
the Blue Parakeet (1)

Women in Church Ministries 4

In one of my classes I asked students to read 1 Timothy 2:8–15 and isolate the commands. (I list seven basic commands below.) Then I asked them to discern whether they thought we should or should not practice that command today. Finally, I asked them then to state why they thought the way they did. Here is the passage; you can do the same assignment with us:

> Therefore I want the men everywhere to pray, lifting up holy hands without anger or disputing. I also want the women to dress modestly, with decency and propriety, adorning themselves, not with elaborate hairstyles or gold or pearls or expensive clothes, but with good deeds, appropriate for women who profess to worship God.
>
> A woman should learn in quietness and full submission. I do not permit a woman to teach or to assume authority over a man; she must be quiet. For Adam was formed first, then Eve. And Adam was not the one deceived; it was the woman who was deceived and became a sinner. But women will be saved through childbearing—if they continue in faith, love and holiness with propriety.

We break the passage into seven basic commands. You can tick off the ones you think are "for today" as stated by Paul.

☐ 1. Males should pray with their hands lifted up (2:8).

No students thought men had to lift their hands when they prayed.

☐ 2. Males should pray without anger or disputing (2:8).

Every student in the class thought men should pray without getting themselves into angry moods and arguments.

☐ 3. Women should dress modestly (2:9).

Two students balked at what "modestly" means in verse 9. They didn't think braiding hair, wearing gold and pearls, or dressing up in expensive clothes is how we define modesty today. But both of these students, Corey and Russell, thought modesty was a good thing. In short, they had a "that was then, but this is now" approach to this passage, and they thought modesty's meaning differs from culture to culture. I asked the females to comment on what "immodest" means today. One commented that a low top was immodest while another said that a top baring one's belly was immodest. Most seemed to agree. I asked males to comment on "immodest" for males. A one-word comment from the back of the class said it all, "Spandex!" We moved to the next point.

☐ 4. Women should not have elaborate hairstyles or wear gold or pearls or expensive clothing (2:9).

The class was divided: twenty-five thought these commands were for today but nineteen thought they were not. Most students thought women should not overdress, but not all were convinced Paul's specific commands were transferable to our world.

☐ 5. Women should have good deeds (2:10).

Every student agreed with Paul.

☐ 6. Women should be silent and quiet (2:11, 12).

Not a single student in the class stated that he or she agreed with Paul on this command. I suspect a few students did agree with this command of Paul's but did not want to endure stares and glares. The same result and observation applies for the last one.

☐ 7. Women should not teach or have authority (2:12).

Whether these numbers of no-silence-for-women are precise or not, the overwhelming majority of the students in this class thought there should be no such restrictions on women today. We could get into a number of issues here, including whether or not this class is typical and the like, but we are not striving for a scientific poll or for accurate numbers. What these students reveal is not at all unusual today; many don't think some of these inspired words of Paul are for today.

But many others do. They think blue parakeets (women) should be silent. We enter now into a minefield of debate. It is impossible for me to discuss each issue, so I will streamline this discussion as a positive explanation of why I think this passage teaches silence *only for women who have not yet been taught*. Once these untaught women are taught, they can sing like the other blue parakeets in the Bible.

A Troubling Irony

We have already sketched some passages in the story of the Bible where we discover the presence of women in leadership and public ministries. I have called these passages the WDWD passages. Now for a theoretical point with enormous significance for women in ministry: some believe the silencing passages should control the WDWD passages. Such persons give any number of reasons, but the point needs to be made clear: such persons believe the silencing passages are permanent and there is no place in the local church today for women prophets, apostles, or leaders or for women to perform any kind of teaching ministry.

There is a troubling irony in this approach, and it concerns whether we Christians are to live under the conditions of the fall or under the conditions of the new creation, whether we are to emphasize otherness or oneness. To explain this, I want to remind you again of the words in Genesis 3:16: "Your desire will be for your husband, and he will rule over you." These words are not an ironclad rule for the rest of history.

Sadly, some think Genesis 3:16 is a *prescription* for the relationship of women and men for all time. Instead of a prescription, these two lines are a *prediction* of the fallen desire of fallen women and fallen men in a fallen condition in a fallen world. Fallen women yearn to dominate the man, and fallen men yearn to dominate women.[1] The desire to dominate is a broken desire. The redeemed desire is to love in mutuality. This verse in Genesis 3, in other words, predicts a struggle of fallen wills; they don't prescribe how we are *supposed* to live.

Genesis 3:16 speaks of fallen humans seeking to control other people. But the fall is not the last word in the Bible, and surely the Song of Songs is a profound example of Israelites finding a better way than what is found in Genesis 3:16. Even more for the Christian we have to factor in new creation, the day God began to renew all things in Jesus Christ and in the gift of the Holy Spirit.

Here is the most important verse in the Bible about new creation: "Therefore, if anyone is in Christ, the new creation has come: The old has gone, the new is here!" (2 Corinthians 5:17). Christian men and women are to live a life that moves beyond the fall, beyond the battle of wills. If new creation does anything, it unleashes the power to undo the fall in our world. I cannot emphasize this enough: the story of the Bible is the story of new creation in Christ. The words of Genesis 3:16, to put the matter directly, are overcome in new creation. These words in Genesis 3:16 are not words for anyone other than unredeemed, fallen women and men. Newly created followers of Christ can find a better way in mutuality. Paul teaches that we are all "one in Christ" and that in Christ there is "neither male nor female" (Galatians 3:28).

Now for the troubling irony: seeking to control or limit the applicability of the WDWD passages by appealing to the silencing passages illustrates the fall, not the new creation. When men seek to control women by silencing them permanently in the church, we stand face-to-face with a contradiction of the very thing the new creation is designed to accomplish: to undo the fall. What we see in this desire to silence women is the desire to rule over women, a desire that pertains to the fall, not to the new creation. What the Spirit does when the Spirit is present is to release and liberate humans from their fallen condition so that God's will can be completely done. The Spirit creates mutuality. Always.

A Brief Reminder

So, when we come upon the two silencing passages, we need to learn to read them out of the story of the Bible. We need to remind ourselves of this:

women in the Old Testament exercised leadership;
women in the Old Testament spoke for God as prophets;
women in the New Testament era were gifted by God's Spirit for
    such things as teaching and leading; and
new creation begins to undo the fall, which means that men and
    women are drawn back into being "one" in Christ.

Even if the Bible's WDWD actions by women were exceptional instead of the norm, God has always raised up women with such gifts. I do think someone could explain the Old Testament WDWD passage as exceptions to the norm, but there's more going on than exceptions in the New Testament. Something new is happening with women in the New Testament.

Another Silenced Blue Parakeet Passage

One of the most significant passages about women in church ministries is often completely ignored, and I'm asking you to drink in what this text says. The plot in the Bible's story reveals that the messianic era would release the Spirit so that *women would also be gifted to exercise prophecy and leadership in the churches.* Just pick up your Bible and open it to Acts 2. When the Spirit fell upon the Pentecostal assembly, including Mary and other women, Peter said:

This is what was spoken by the prophet Joel:

"*In the last days, God says,*
I will pour out my Spirit on all people.
Your sons and daughters will prophesy,
your young men will see visions,
your old men will dream dreams.
Even on my servants, both men and women,
I will pour out my Spirit in those days,
and they will prophesy." (Acts 2:16–18, emphasis added)

Pentecost was the day the music of the fall died and the day new creation music began to be sung. It doesn't take but a lazy reading of Acts 2 to see that something big and something new was happening, and that bigness and that newness included women. Pentecost, so the Bible tells us, leads us to think of an *increase* in women's capacities to minister, not a decrease. Women's ministries *expand* as the Bible's plot moves forward; they do not shrink. Many today have shrunk the role of women in ministries; this flat-out contradicts the direction of the Bible's plot.

We must return to the point made in the previous chapters. We must ask WDWD, what did women do? We must ask about how the Story moves forward in the Bible. This kind of Bible reading means that when we read about women being silenced in Paul, you and I are drawn into a decision. Either we see Paul contradicting the way God has used women in the Story or we are being asked to see the silence as a special kind of silence. That is the point we will sketch out for both 1 Corinthians 14:34–35 and 1 Timothy 2:8–15.

Silencing Women at Corinth

The reason some believe in silencing women begins with 1 Corinthians 14:34–35.[2] Here are Paul's words:

> Women should remain silent in the churches. They are not allowed to speak, but must be in submission, as the law says. If they want to inquire about something, they should ask their own husbands at home; for it is disgraceful for a woman to speak in the church.

Knowing what we know from our WDWD reading about the role of women in the early churches, we are surprised that Paul would say "women should remain silent in the churches." Furthermore, Paul himself gives instructions on women prophesying in the churches in this same letter to the Corinthians. One can't prophesy (or pray) in public and remain completely silent; prophesying means talking in public! At 1 Corinthians 11, Paul says this about women in public church gatherings: "But every woman who *prays or prophesies* with her head uncovered dishonors her head—it is the same as having her head shaved" (11:5, emphasis added). And we know from the book of Acts that women exercised the gift of prophecy in the churches. Peter saw this as a fulfillment of the prophet Joel (Acts 2:17–18; 21:9).

So, yes, we are surprised by the sudden appearance of a command for silence for women. Many of us, when reading these words about silence after we have absorbed the Story, ask this: If women did what we have already seen they did (WDWDs) and if Paul offers clear directions on how women should exercise their gift of prophecy in public gatherings, how can he suddenly say women should "remain silent"? Has he not contradicted himself? A shallow reading of the Story points a long finger at Paul's inconsistency. Reading the Bible as Story, however, discerns what Paul was saying in a very specific circumstance. So, how do we explain 1 Corinthians 14?

Many today believe that Paul's silencing of women is a *special kind of silencing*. Paul is not totally silencing women; that would contradict his own teaching and the WDWDs of the Bible. We are not completely sure what kind of special silence he has in mind, so let me sketch three options. Some think Paul prohibits women from *evaluating prophesies*. Others think Paul is asking women to be silent when it comes to *speaking in or interpreting tongues*, another special concern in this passage. The third option comes from Craig Keener, an expert scholar on the historical background to the New Testament, who keenly observes that Paul's own words clarifies this best. Paul silences women in regard to *asking questions*: "If they want *to inquire about something*, they should ask their own husbands [if they are married] at home; for it is disgraceful for a woman to speak [inquire about something they don't yet understand] in the church."[3] I think Keener gets this one right.

Why would Paul restrict the asking of questions? The best answer is because these women were not yet educated theologically or biblically as well as the men. (That's another discussion.) When these women heard what was being said, they had questions. Paul thinks those sorts of questions should be asked elsewhere, probably because it interrupted the service. This conclusion has significant implications. Paul's silencing of women at Corinth is then only a *temporary* silencing. Once the women with questions had been educated, they would be permitted then to ask questions in the gatherings of Christians.

An implication of Paul's statements is the responsibility of Christian men and leaders to educate women, and this would have stood out in the ancient world as a progressive ideal. As Keener states it, Paul "supports learning before speaking." He adds that such an educational process would not "prohibit women in very different cultural settings from speaking God's word." Furthermore, we must pay special attention to the fact that women today are not uneducated—in fact, some male pastors are! This passage testifies to the importance of education — of knowing the Bible and theology and having pastoral gifts and skills — and once those basics are met, anyone with gifts should be encouraged to use their gifts.

This message in 1 Corinthians 14 is completely explored in 1 Timothy 2. So, let's look at this most famous of silencing passages.

Silencing the Women at Ephesus

Because Paul's instruction for the elders in Ephesus (note that Timothy was in Ephesus when Paul wrote this letter to him; see 1 Timothy 1:3) to silence women is a blue parakeet passage used by some to silence blue parakeets (women), and because many think such a view is politically incorrect, the passage has itself become a blue parakeet and has been silenced by both sides!

A Brief Sketch

I begin with a brief summary of 1 Timothy 2:9 – 15. In this sketch I will anticipate some points I will clarify a little later.[4] Before doing so, let me call attention to the significance of this passage in the history of the church — in particular, to its significance in the shaping of how the Great Tradition has understood the role of women in church ministries. This passage is number one in restricting women's ministries from public teaching and preaching. In this and the next chapter I will push against that Tradition. But because this passage has had such an enormous impact, I am asking you to plow through it with me.

Modesty (1 Timothy 2:9 – 10)

I also want the women to dress modestly, with decency and propriety, adorning themselves, not with elaborate hairstyles or gold or pearls or expensive clothes, but with good deeds, appropriate for women who profess to worship God.

First, Paul expects the women to whom he is speaking to dress modestly; by that he means they are not to dress elaborately or seductively and are to focus their attention on "good deeds." The reason for this has to do with the respectability of the gospel and the church and, as we will explain in the next chapter, Paul is concerned with the influence of the new Roman women who threatened the reputation of the gospel.

Learning before Teaching (1 Timothy 2:11–12)

A woman should learn in quietness and full submission. I do not permit a woman to teach or to assume authority over a man; she must be quiet.

Second, and I embolden these verses because they are our concern here, Paul expects women first to learn in quietness and full submission to those who know, and only then does he say they are not to teach or exercise authority. *Learning* women — and this now sounds like 1 Corinthians 14 — are to "be quiet." Paul does not say that women are always to sit in the learning posture and never to be teachers; he does not say they are forever to remain silent, for that would contradict the WDWD passages and practices in the early churches.

Adam and Eve (1 Timothy 2:13–14)

For Adam was formed first, then Eve. And Adam was not the one deceived; it was the woman who was deceived and became a sinner.

Third, in these two verses Paul anchors the silencing of unlearned women in two points: (1) Adam was "formed first" and (2) Eve was first to be deceived. These two statements surprise the reader. It is entirely possible Paul is responding to the new Roman women, whom we will describe in the next chapter. These new Roman women could have been claiming that the gender order should be reversed, with women subordinating men, and that the original creation was first females and then males.

We cannot be sure why Paul says what he says here. However one interprets these verses—and let's be honest enough to say they are difficult—if we make them an inflexible rule that women should always be silent, we have a flat-out contradiction to the Story of the Bible, to the practices of Priscilla and Junia and Phoebe, and to Paul himself. My personal opinion is that Paul is responding to the claims of new Roman women that women were superior to men.

Childbearing and Salvation (1 Timothy 2:15)

> But women will be saved through childbearing—if they continue
> in faith, love and holiness with propriety.

Fourth, Paul continues to say that if women—and here he is speaking to married women—continue in the faith, they will be "saved through childbearing." Once again, no one knows for certain what this verse means. Many today think the verse has something to do with the new Roman women's avoidance of marriage while others also suggest that he is responding to the growing attraction on the part of the new Roman women to terminate their pregnancies. Yes, if this is so, we may have an allusion to abortion in the New Testament. Paul discerns that these Christian (and married) women need to know that being married and being mothers are worthy vocations for women. (By the way, Paul is not here advocating that all women must be married.)

We must now examine the cultural context of Paul so we can discern both what he was saying in his day and in his way and how we can live this out in our day and in our way.

Chapter 15

Silencing
the Blue Parakeet (2)

Women in Church Ministries 5

Kris and I once participated in a church where some women wore "head coverings" whenever we assembled for worship and teaching. These women (and their husbands) believed they were following Paul's instructions in 1 Corinthians 11:6, which reads: "For if a woman does not cover her head, she might as well have her hair cut off; but if it is a disgrace for a woman to have her hair cut off or her head shaved, then she should cover her head."

There was some discussion, because of a book in the 1980s, about whether Paul meant a cloth head covering or just long hair drawn up over the head. More importantly, many of us had discerned a more historical intent to Paul's words. We knew the research that suggested that the women at Corinth were "letting their hair hang down." We knew that unkempt hair was how prostitutes dressed. So, we discerned that Paul was concerned about how this appearance by women would impact the reputation of the gospel. These loose-haired women, in Paul's opinion, gave off the suggestion that the Christian gatherings were sexual in nature.

One of my closest friends, and a brilliant scholar of the New

Testament, made this observation about the situation at our church in light of the context of Paul's words: "Scot, some at your church don't seem willing to ask if insisting on head coverings might do *the opposite of what Paul was actually doing.*" In other words, insisting on head coverings does as much (if not more) damage to the gospel today as *not* wearing head coverings did in the first century! How so? If we demand women do something so totally contrary to culture that non-Christians are offended or turned off, we should reconsider what we are doing. Paul didn't want the dress of Christian women to bring a bad name to the gospel, so he asked them to wear head coverings; by contrast, demanding women to wear head coverings in our world may do the very same damage to the gospel. (In fact, I'm quite sure it would.)

My friend was right. Context is everything. Knowing context permits deeper and wiser discernment. So what was the historical context to Paul's words in 1 Timothy 2:9 – 15?

New Roman Women in Ephesus:
Dress, Public Discourse, Anti-Marriage

When Paul wrote his letters to the Christians in Corinth and to Timothy in Ephesus, *a gender and sexual revolution was observable in many of the major cities of the Roman Empire.* What many today are calling the "new Roman woman" describes an aggressive, confrontational public presence on the part of women during the very time Paul was writing these letters. Here are the characteristics, and you can look at Appendix 4 for a specific text that illustrates the sort of thing Paul was probably referring to. Three features of the new Roman woman set our passage in its historical context.

First, the new Roman woman was expressing her newfound freedoms in *immodest, sexually provocative, and extravagant dress.* Rome was not terribly conservative, but these women were flouting even the limits of the Romans.

Second, the new Roman woman was noted for *snatching the podium for public addresses and teaching* (see Appendix 5 for a text where men complain about educated women).

Third, especially in Ephesus, alongside the presence of the new Roman woman was *the Artemis religious fertility cult*. This worship cult not only favored the freedom of women in public religion as did the new Roman woman movement, but it also surrounded these worshipers with eunuch (castrated male) priests. Part of their worship was the elimination of normal sexual relations; these women despised marriage and childbearing and childrearing. Furthermore, this fertility cult extended their sexual and gender freedoms into open practices of abortion and contraception.[1]

The Roman Empire was hardly prudish when it came to dress codes, but this new Roman woman movement alarmed the establishment. Caesar Augustus, for instance, passed laws legislating what respectable women were to wear and how prostitutes and adulteresses were to dress. Naturally, these laws were debated and they were also flouted by the new Roman woman.[2] But our concern is with Paul and the women in Ephesus, who were under Timothy's leadership. Paul was all for Spirit-led gifts on the part of women — a liberating impulse on his part. But he had deep concerns when the influence of the new Roman woman began to jeopardize the holiness of the Christian church. Some critics of the church were apparently suggesting that the church was little more than a fertility cult.

This is the context for Paul's statements in 1 Timothy 2:9 – 15. The big point Paul makes is not to "keep the women silent" but to "teach the women." His principle was "learning before teaching." If I am asked how this text "applies" to our modern world, I would discern that we need "learning before teaching." And I would also discern something Paul didn't think he needed to say: men, too, need learning before teaching. Why? Because in that day men were more privileged in education than women. It's that simple. Any reading of the Bible, especially a passage like this, that doesn't recognize male privilege will not come to terms with the social codes in the text.

Now let's make a connection that readers of 1 Timothy 2 do not make often enough. A major clue to reading 1 Timothy 2 is found in the very same letter — in 1 Timothy 5.

Problems in the Churches at Ephesus

Paul's letter to Timothy is laced together with two strings — the danger of false teaching and the need for orthodox teaching. Of particular concern to Paul was a group of young widows whom we meet directly in 1 Timothy 5:11 – 14. Paul's words there, which can strike the modern reader as terribly simplistic, are directed to a specific group of young widows who had behavior issues. When Paul silences women in 1 Timothy 2, he is almost certainly silencing especially the widows we find in chapter 5, and I would encourage you to read 1 Timothy 2 and 5 in comparison. Below are the words of Paul from 1 Timothy 5 about some young widows, and we need to read each word carefully because themes we have just touched appear over and over.

Sensuality among the Younger Widows (1 Timothy 5:11 – 12)

As for younger widows, do not put them on such a [widow] list. For when their *sensual desires* overcome their dedication to Christ, they want to marry. Thus they bring judgment on themselves, because they have broken their first pledge [of faith in Christ]. (emphasis added)

The language Paul uses for these women is noteworthy: he is describing a widow who has developed a promiscuous, sexual lifestyle and who is thus abandoning the faith. These are not ordinary Christian young widows; these widows are a group of young women with a well-known reputation of public sexuality. This sounds very much like the new Roman woman. Their sexual lifestyle is not the whole point, and it is the next verse that shows us that the women of chapter 2 are in view.

Busybody Teachers (1 Timothy 5:13)

Besides, they get into the habit of being idle and going about from house to house. And not only do they become idlers, but also busybodies who talk nonsense, saying things they ought not to.

If we set these words in the new Roman woman context, and if we remember what we read in 1 Timothy 2:9 – 15, we will see that 1 Timothy 5 is referring to young widows who, because they are not yet theologically formed, are being accused by Paul of idling and busybodying. *What* they were doing — visiting friends — is not Paul's concern. What they were *saying and teaching* was Paul's concern.

The Virtue of Marriage (1 Timothy 5:14)

So I counsel younger widows to marry, to have children, to manage their homes and to give the enemy no opportunity for slander.

This verse sounds yet again like 1 Timothy 2:15: "But women will be saved through childbearing — if they continue in faith, love and holiness with propriety." I doubt very much that Paul is demanding that all women everywhere marry, have children, and manage their homes. But if we factor in the new Roman woman's desire to end marriage and childbearing and to pursue instead a sexually promiscuous life, Paul is countering those ideas with the virtue of marriage and managing a home.

Summary

Let me now sum all this up, for it is this context that gives rise to the silencing of women: a new group of Roman women were advocating counter-Christian ideas. Paul was concerned about the reputation of the gospel and the respectability of Christian women for fear they might be associated with the offensive side of such behaviors. So Paul turns to the women in Ephesus — in particular, to a group of young widows. He urges them to live a life of holiness and to learn before they start teaching.

We are thus led to the conclusion that when Paul asks women to be silent in 1 Timothy 2, he is not talking about ordinary Christian women; rather, he has a specific group of women in mind. His concern is with some untrained, morally loose, young widows, who, because they are theologically unformed, are teaching unorthodox ideas. Paul does not advocate, then, that women should not teach but that they should learn sound theology before they teach.

Context is everything, and in this case a little knowledge of the Roman world and a glance at 1 Timothy 5 provides all we need. Even if we lacked knowledge about the new Roman woman, what Paul says about widows in 1 Timothy 5 tells us about all we need to know to make clear sense of 1 Timothy 2.

It's All in Our Passage!

First Timothy 2:9–15 is aimed directly at women, especially the young widows, who are following the new Roman woman in public behaviors and who don't know enough theology to teach sound doctrine.

Paul, ever vigilant about the reputation of the gospel, urges these women to wear modest clothing, to exercise sexual restraint, and to do good deeds. But, *more than that*—and often ignored—Paul utters something that should completely shift the focus of this passage: "A woman should *learn* in quietness and full submission" (1 Timothy 2:11, emphasis added). Paul's focus here is not on what women *cannot* do, which unfortunately is how the silencers of blue parakeets read this passage, but on what these women must do: *learn*. He is not concerned with silence in general but with *silence in order to learn*. In light of the Story and of how we have answered WDWD, we conclude that the silence Paul talks about in both 1 Corinthians 14 and 1 Timothy 2 is a temporary silence—temporary until these women have learned.

The teaching that Paul prohibits, then, is unorthodox theology. Until these young women are informed and until they are formed in character, they need to be learners. (The same can be said for men, who, in Paul's world, had more opportunities to learn.) So, when Paul says they need to "*learn* in quietness and full submission," he is speaking here of deference to the wise teachers, the elders, who are orthodox and godly, not to a permanent condition of utter silence. Once they learn, they will be ready to teach and to travel from house church to house church to impart wisdom and demonstrate godliness.

Paul's two comments about silence are actually consistent, then, with the story and plot of the Bible. Women, who have always been gifted by God to speak for God and to lead God's people, were doing just those things in Paul's churches. But women who had not yet learned Bible and theology or who had not yet learned how to live a Christian life were not to become teachers until they had learned orthodox theology.

What drives 1 Corinthians 14 and 1 Timothy 2 is a principle that much of the church tradition has nearly smothered when it comes to women: "Learning precedes teaching." When churches today ask leaders questions about the Bible and theology and when pastoral search committees ask about the education of candidates, they are living out what Paul was saying in these two passages.

What about Scripture? What about Today?

Some are surprised by what they learn when they read explanations like this. Some want to throw away their Bibles and say, "Only the experts can do this!" Some find liberation. Some say they almost threw away their Bible until they learned the Bible, too, emerged out of a context. They say, "Show me how to do this on my own!"

Both of these groups of people believe in the Bible.

Perhaps you disagree with my reading of these silencing passages. Let me then put it another way. We can at least begin with two basic options: *either* we have a general prohibition of women teaching and leading *with some exceptions* (the hierarchical view, *through* the many layers of church tradition), *or* we have the possibility of women teaching and leading *with some restrictions* (the mutuality view, *with* [and perhaps *against*] tradition). There is no ground, however, for total silencing of women in the church.

When we consider these two options, does it not strike you that, at the very least, women can *sometimes* teach and lead? *In the Bible, women did lead and women did teach.* Some today want to take back what women did, while others (I include myself here) want to expand what women can do today because we live in a different world. Those who are taking back the teaching and leading ministries of women are fighting the Bible, not embracing it. They are silencing blue parakeets. They are saying, "We know what women did in the Bible, but that's not for today!" Let me ask you a question: Is this being biblical? Is this following the clear expansion of ministries from Pentecost on? I believe a post-Pentecost reading of the Bible encourages us to give the blue parakeets a chance to sing!

You might ask me, "Why do you think we can expand the ministries of women?" Very simply: the plot of the Bible, the story of the Bible, and the behaviors of women in that Plot and Story reveal to me an increasing expansion of women in church ministries. Some of the restrictions were based on respectability and culture. If those restrictions have changed, then I see no reason to limit the ministries of women to the sensibilities and cultures of that time. God spoke in those days in those ways, and I believe he is speaking in our days in our ways.

But I have no desire here to suggest this expansion of the role of women is for all in all places. I return to Phil Towner's observations—and here he brings in the unique combination of not only an expertise on our text but also decades of experience on the mission field. Phil and I generally agree on how to read this passage. But he offers us this caution: "What this means for Christianity in traditional Asian or Muslim contexts is that too much too fast could endanger the church's witness and credibility. But in much of the Western world, too little too slow could neutralize the church's impact in society just as effectively."[3]

What we need is discernment.

The Pauline Principle of Discernment

If any words in the Bible capture the essence of this book, they can be found in the first letter Paul sent off to the Corinthians. What I'm not sure we always ponder, perhaps because it will attract a yard full of blue parakeets, is just how creative, liberating, and forward-looking this passage is. Here are Paul's words from 1 Corinthians 9:19 – 23:

> Though I am free and belong to no one, I have made myself a slave to everyone, to win as many as possible. To the Jews I became like a Jew, to win the Jews. To those under the law I became like one under the law (though I myself am not under the law), so as to win those under the law. To those not having the law I became like one not having the law (though I am not free from God's law but am under Christ's law), so as to win those not having the law. To the weak I became weak, to win the weak. I have become all things to all people so that by all possible means I might save some. I do all this for the sake of the gospel, that I may share in its blessings.

Here's a question I hope you can toss around with your friends: Do you think Paul would have put women "behind the pulpit" if it would have been advantageous "for the sake of gospel"? I believe Paul would exhort us to open the cages and let the blue parakeets fly and let them sing.

What Paul states in 1 Corinthians 9 forms the core of how we have to learn to read the Bible. Paul himself adapted the gospel to every situation he encountered: a Jewish expression for Jews, a Gentile expression for Gentiles, and a philosopher's approach when on the Areopagus (Acts 17). What Paul did is simple: he knew the Story and the Plot, he listened to God and was open to the Spirit, and he discerned how to live out that gospel and speak that gospel into each cultural setting. Paul's mode was renewing and always renewing.

Recently in a class session of college students, I sketched three options we have in reading the Bible (the three views I sketched in chapter 2): read and retrieve it all, read the Bible *through* tradition, and read the

Bible *with* tradition (including challenging the tradition). After class, a fine student pressed me, with intellectual articulation and heartfelt passion, that if we choose the third option we are led to hundreds of views with no real unity. How can we let everyone read the Bible for themselves? Won't that lead to millions of readings?

My response? No, it won't lead to millions of readings, but it will lead to many readings. Culturally shaped readings of the Bible and culturally shaped expressions of the gospel are exactly what Paul did and wanted. That's exactly what Peter and Hebrews and John and James and the others were doing. Culturally shaped readings and expressions of the gospel are the way it has been, is, and always will be. In fact, I believe that gospel adaptation for every culture, for every church, and for every Christian is precisely why God gave us the Bible. The Bible shows us how.

The Waterslide Again

God has given us his Word, the Bible. That Word provides for us the gospel. That gospel is the waterslide, banked on one side by the Bible's canon and banked on the other side by the wisdom of the church, the Great Tradition. The water running down the slide is the Holy Spirit. We are called to enter the slide at the top (Genesis) and ride it all the way down—safely protected by canon and conversation with Tradition—to the end (Revelation). If we ride it properly, wetted down as we are by the Holy Spirit and cheered on by the communion of saints, we will land in the water where we need to be—in our day and in our way.

F. F. Bruce

In the spring of 1981, as a doctoral student in Nottingham England, I piled Kris and our two kids, Laura and Lukas, into our small car and drove to Buxton. Professor F. F. Bruce, perhaps the most widely known evangelical scholar of the previous generation and a specialist on Paul, had invited our family to his home for late-afternoon tea. When we arrived, we were welcomed into the home by Professor Bruce, and we sat in the living room for about two hours. During that time our son managed to spill a glass of orange squash on the Bruce's rug, which Professor Bruce dismissed with a "whatever can be spilled has been spilled on that rug."

During a break, as Kris was talking to Mrs. Bruce, I asked Professor Bruce a question that I had stored up for him (and I repeat our conversation from my memory): "Professor Bruce, what do you think of women's ordination?"

"I don't think the New Testament talks about ordination," he replied.

"What about the silencing passages of Paul on women?" I asked.

"I think Paul would roll over in his grave if he knew we were turning his letters into *torah*."

Wow! I thought. *That's a good point to think about.* Thereupon I asked a question that he answered in such a way that it reshaped my thinking: "What do you think, then, about women in church ministries?"

Professor Bruce's answer was as Pauline as Paul was: "I'm for whatever God's Spirit grants women gifts to do."

So am I. Let the blue parakeets sing!

Now What?

We've covered lots of ground in *The Blue Parakeet*, but that is only because the question — "How then do we read the Bible?" — deserves our attention. There are enough passages in the Bible — and I began to sense this when I was a young Christian — that, when we read them, make us think all over again about how we are reading the Bible. I call these passages the "blue parakeet passages."

Blue parakeet passages are oddities in the Bible that we prefer to cage and silence rather than to permit into our sacred mental gardens. If we are honest, blue parakeet passages often threaten us, call into question our traditional way of reading the Bible, and summon us back to the Bible to rethink how we read the Bible. Though we could have chosen other themes or ideas, the issue of women in church ministries was our test case for how we both read the Bible and how we bring it into our world.

So, how then do we read the Bible? I'd like to sum up what this book has said.

The Big Temptation

Many of us will be tempted to take the shortcuts when we read the Bible and especially when we encounter a blue parakeet passage. Instead of reading each passage in its storied context, we will zoom in on getting out of the Bible what we want. Once again, the shortcuts we have all learned in reading the Bible are:

- to treat the Bible as a collection of laws
- to treat the Bible as a collection of blessings and promises
- to treat the Bible as a Rohrschach inkblot onto which we can project our own ideas
- to treat the Bible as a giant puzzle that we are to puzzle together
- to treat one of the Bible's authors as a Maestro

We have only one other genuine option, to read the Bible from front to back as Story. Before we summarize what we said about the Story, let's see what's wrong with each of these shortcuts. Yes, strategy will guide us to something true about the Bible: there are laws, there are blessings and promises, there are moments when we see in the Bible something about our own lives, there are parts of the Bible that we are challenged to puzzle together, and there are Maestros — many of them. But, there are problems with each of these:

- The Bible is more than laws, and each law is connected to its context.
- The Bible is more than blessings and promises; there are some warnings and threats as well.
- The Bible is something that comes to us from God and not something onto which we can impose our wishes and desires.
- The Bible is a story to be read, not a divinely scattered puzzle to be pieced together into a system that makes sense of it all.
- The Bible is a collection of wiki-stories of the Story, and each author, each Maestro, is but one voice at the table.

It is tempting to return to the safety of our former reading habits. But if we listen to the blue parakeet passages in the Bible, which are there at God's discretion, and if we think about how we are reading them, the Bible somehow unfolds before our eyes as a brilliant Story.

The Story

God chose to give us a collection of books, what I call wiki-stories of the Story, and together these books form into God's story with us and God's story for us. Acts 7 is a good example of how to read the Bible as Story even though Stephen's speech in Acts 7 is only one wiki-story of the Story. Again, each author in the Bible is a wiki-storyteller and each book is then a wiki-story, one story in the ongoing development of the big story. These are the major elements of that story:

1. God and creation
2. Adam and Eve as Eikons who crack the Eikon
3. God's covenant community, where humans are restored to God, self, others, and the world
4. Jesus Christ, who is the Story and in whose story we are to live
5. the church as Jesus' covenant community
6. the consummation, when all the designs of our Creator God will finally be realized forever and ever

What we discover in reading the Bible is that each telling of the Story, each wiki-story, was a Spirit-inspired telling of the Story in each person's day in each person's way. God spoke through Moses in Moses' ways for Moses' days, through David in David's ways for David's days, through Jesus in Jesus' ways for Jesus' days, and through John in John's ways for John's days. God always speaks a "contemporary" word. The genius of the Bible is the continuity of the Story as each generation learns to speak it afresh in its days and in its ways.

Furthermore, each wiki-storyteller, each author in the Bible, tells a story that will lead us to the person of the Story: Jesus Christ. As Moses and Isaiah look forward to that person, so Paul and Peter and Hebrews look back to that person. Jesus Christ, then, is the goal and the center of each wiki-story.

This leads me to a major strategy in reading the Bible. Every author in the Bible was divinely directed through God's Spirit to tell a true story of the one Story. This means that our task in reading the Bible is to "map" the elements of the Story in each wiki-story. If we keep our eyes on the six elements of the Story as outlined above, we will have all we need for reading the Bible. These six elements govern the story of the Bible and each book focuses on one or more of these elements.

Living Out the Story Today

We must never make the mistake of exalting the paper on which the Bible is written over the person who puts the words on that paper. Our relationship to the Bible is actually, if we are properly engaged, a relationship with the God of the Bible. God gave us the Bible as a person who speaks to you and me as persons through words. God gave us the Bible so we could be transformed and bring glory to him by living out a life in this world that God designs for us. How do we do this?

We are summoned by the God who speaks to us in the Bible to *listen* to God speak, to *live out* what God directs us to live out, and to *discern how* to live out the Story in our own day. One way of saying all of this can be found in Moses' original words and in what I call the Jesus Creed version of Moses' words: we are to love God and to love others. If we love God and love others, we will listen to God in the Bible, live out what God calls us to live out, and discern how to live out the Story in our world today. Discernment, of course, calls for some special attention.

I used the image of the waterslide in this book for how we discern how to live today. Graced by the watery gift of the Spirit, we sit on the gospel and are constrained by the Bible and guided by the wise mentors of the church (reading the Bible *with* tradition), and we ride this all so we can land in our world with a gospel for our day shaped in our way. What we need is two things if we are to do this well.

First, we need to be mastered by the *Story* by reading the Bible so deeply that its story becomes our story. If we let that story become our story, we will inhabit the Bible's very own story. Now, let me remind us that it is not simply this story that masters us but the God of that story. By indwelling the story of the Bible, we indwell the God who tells that story.

Second, together as God's people we are to so inhabit the Story that we can *discern* how to live in our world. Our calling is to live out the ageless Story in our world. To do this we have to bring back the Spirit of God into our interpretation of the Bible. We read the Bible with all the tools of history and language that we can muster, but a proper reading of the Bible is attended by the Spirit, who will transform us, guide us, and give us discernment to know how to live in our world.

What Now?

Reading the Bible as Story teaches us to look forward by looking to our past. It teaches us to go back to that story so we know how to go forward in our world. We must not be afraid of where God will lead us as we live out this story today, just as David and Isaiah and Jesus and Paul and Peter were unafraid where God might lead them. We cannot think that we will find security by going back and staying in the past. We cannot think that our task is complete once we've figured what Paul or Peter meant when they spoke the gospel in their world. Instead, we are given a pattern of discernment in the Bible, a pattern that flows directly out of the Story, to listen to what God said in that world so we can know what God is saying to us through our world. So we can know what God wants us to say about that story to our world — in our world's ways.

If the Bible does anything for us as we read it as Story, it gives us the confidence to face the future with the good news about Jesus Christ in the power of the Spirit. God's Spirit, the Story tells us, is with us to guide us and to give us discernment.

The story of the Bible is not only the story of our past, it is the story for our future.

After Words

I teach the Bible, and as my friend and colleague Brad Nassif and I often remind ourselves, not only do we teach the Bible but this is our job. I could not have dreamt of a better job or of a better opportunity than having colleagues like Brad — such as Boaz Johnson, Joel Willitts, Ginny Olson, and Jim Dekker.

This teaching kind of life has given me many good friends, fellow Bible readers who teach me and probe me. Those who have read parts of this book or who have listened to me talk about it, besides the wonderful crowd we had at the National Pastor's Convention in San Diego in February of 2008, include my longtime friend Joe Modica and his colleague, Dwight Peterson, at Eastern University, where I was invited one evening for a public conversation about the contents of this book. Their questions pushed me to reshape parts of this book.

I wish to mention others who, through conversation or reading some or all of this manuscript, have helped me shape my thoughts more accurately: Norton Herbst and Jason Malec, both at North Point in Atlanta, J. R. Briggs, Roseanne Sension, Nancy Beach at Willow Creek Community Church, Nancy Ortberg, Cheryl Hatch, Doreen and Mark Olson, Julie Clawson, Kent and Phyllis Palmer, and Peter Chang and Kathy Khang. I cannot fail to mention Greg Clark, my colleague, with whom I have shared discussions about hermeneutics—the art of reading the Bible—for fifteen years.

John Raymond of Zondervan is not only my editor, but his father was my college basketball coach; John himself was our "manager" as a teenager, and he has been a friend to me and Kris and our kids for decades. I am grateful for John. In a strange turn of fate, I have ceased reading his papers and he is now reading mine! I am grateful to my agent, Greg Daniel of the Daniel Literary Group, for his wisdom and advice on this manuscript. Both John and Greg made this a much better book.

Kris refers to books like this one as my "readable" books. She doesn't read my "unreadable" ones, but books like this one are important to her. She read every chapter, made detailed comments at times, and urged me time and time again to make the book better. She began to refer to one of the chapters in this book as "The Boring Chapter," and so we gave that chapter her words. Without her you might not be holding this book in your hand. Kris has been my best friend and loving wife for more than thirty years. Proverbs 31 doesn't even come close to describing her.

Kris and I chose to dedicate this book to our friend and my former student Cheryl Hatch. Let me put it this way: even if you try to clip the wings or silence the voice of a blue parakeet, somehow her glory and her gifts find a way.

Scot McKnight
Easter 2008

Appendix 1

A Discernment Quiz*

This quiz was an assignment asked of me by Skye Jethani, the editor of *Leadership Journal*. Our initial conversation at a coffee shop generated so many ideas we could not contain them all in one quiz. So we drafted a quiz to see if we could get a conversation going about how we read the Bible and how we "apply" the Bible. For most questions we sensed we could have had ten or more different answers, and scaling our answers proved especially difficult. That quiz also gave some labels connected to scores that generated more controversy than was intended. I have no desire here to label; instead, I have one desire with this quiz: we need to talk more about how we are reading the Bible, and instruments like this are one way of getting us to rethink how we read the Bible. I've eliminated the labels in this edition of the quiz.

On a scale of 1–5, mark the answer that best fits your approach to reading the Bible. If, for example, you fall between response 1 and response 3, give yourself a 2; or between 3 and 5, give yourself a 4. Place your score in the space after the colon. Maybe you want to rewrite the whole question; go ahead. Choose, in other words, the answer that is closest to your own view. What interests me most is getting you and others into a conversation about how we read and apply the Bible.

---

* Originally in *Leadership Journal*

A. The Bible is: _____

    1. God's inspired words in confluence with the authors (genuine dual authorship).

    3. God's inspired words that arise out of a community and then are written down by an author (less author, more community).

    5. Words of an author who speaks out of a community's tradition, but which sacramentally lead us to God.

B. The Bible is: _____

    1. God's exact words for all time.

    3. God's message (instead of exact words) for all time.

    5. God's words and message for that time but need interpretation and contextualization to be lived today.

C. The Bible's words are: _____

    1. Inerrant on everything.

    3. Inerrant only on matters of faith and practice.

    5. Not defined by inerrancy or errancy, which are modernistic categories.

D. The commands in the Old Testament to destroy a village, including women and children, are: _____

    1. Justifiable judgment against sinful, pagan, immoral peoples.

    3. God's ways in the days of the judges (etc.); they are primitive words but people's understanding as divine words for that day.

    5. A barbaric form of war in a primitive society and I wish they weren't in the Bible.

E. The story of Hosea (the prophet) and Gomer (his wife) is: _____

    1. A graphic reality that speaks of God's faithfulness and Israel's infidelity.

    3. A parable (since, for example, God would never ask a prophet to marry a prostitute).

    5. An unfortunate image of an ancient prophet that stereotypes women and too easily justifies violence against women.

F. The command of Jesus to wash feet is: _____
   1. To be taken literally, despite near universal neglect in the church.
   3. A first-century observance to be practiced today in other ways.
   5. An ancient custom with no real implication for our world.

G. The gift of prophecy is: _____
   1. Timeless, despite lack of attention in the church today.
   3. An ancient form of communication that is seen today in proclaiming scriptural truths.
   5. No longer needed and dramatically different from today's preaching.

H. Prohibitions of homosexuality in the Bible are: _____
   1. Permanent prohibitions reflecting God's will.
   3. Culturally shaped, still normative, but demanding greater sensitivity today.
   5. A purity-code violation that has been eliminated by Christ.

I. The unity of the Bible is: _____
   1. God's systematic truth that can be discerned by careful study of the Bible.
   3. The gospel call to living by faith that is expressed in a variety of ways by different authors in the Bible.
   5. Not found by imposing on the integrity of each author in the Bible to conform to overarching systems; the unity is in the God who speaks to us today through the Word.

J. The Holy Spirit's role in interpretation is: _____
   1. To guide the individual regardless of what others say.
   3. To guide the individual in tandem/conversation with the church.
   5. To guide the community that can instruct the individual.

K. The injunctions upon women in 1 Timothy 2:9–15 are: _____

   1. Timeless truths and normative for today.

   3. Culturally shaped but, with proper interpretation and transfer, for today; e.g., we can learn from how Paul addressed a situation with uninstructed women in Ephesus.

   5. Needed for early Christians, bound in the first century, but not for today.

L. Careful interpretation of the Bible is: _____

   1. Objective, rational, universal, timeless.

   3. Dialectical, relational, culturally shaped, timely.

   5. Subjective, personal, culturally bound, time specific.

M. The context for reading the Bible is: _____

   1. The individual's sole responsibility.

   3. The individual in conversation with, and respect for, church traditions.

   5. The confessional statement of one's community of faith.

N. Discerning the historical context of a passage is: _____

   1. Unimportant since God speaks to me directly.

   3. Often or sometimes significant in order to grasp meaning.

   5. Necessary and dangerous to avoid in reading the Bible.

O. The Bible: _____

   1. Can be examined and understood without bias.

   3. Can be understood but with bias.

   5. Can be only partially understood by a reader with bias.

P. Capital punishment: _____

   1. Should be practiced today because the Bible teaches it.

   3. Should be examined carefully to determine if it is the best option today; some instances of capital punishment in the Bible are no longer advisable.

   5. As delineated in the Bible pertains to ancient Israel; such practices are no longer useful and should be universally banned.

Q. Tattoos: _____
   1. Are forbidden because of Leviticus 19:28.
   3. Are forbidden in Leviticus as idolatrous marks, which we know from study of the ancient Near East.
   5. Are permissible, because the purity codes are not for Christians today.

R. The requirement of the Jerusalem Council (Acts 15:29) not to eat any meat improperly killed (strangled instead of having the blood drained properly): _____
   1. Is a permanent commandment for all Christians today.
   3. Is for Jewish Christians only.
   5. Is a temporary custom for first-century Jewish Christians and is no longer a concern for Christians.

S. Adultery: _____
   1. Deserves the death penalty, as stated in the Old Testament.
   3. Was not punished by death when Jesus confronted it, and therefore death is not a Christian punishment.
   5. Adultery and divorce were governed by Old Testament laws from a primitive culture, very different from our own; just as these concepts developed within Bible times, our understanding of proper punishment has been improved.

T. Sabbath: _____
   1. Was never eliminated by New Testament writers and should be practiced by Christians (on Saturday).
   3. Developed into a Sunday worship observance for Christians, and Christians should not work on that day.
   5. Turned into Sunday for Christians, who need to worship together (on the weekend, at least) and can work if they think they need to.

Images of Jesus*

This test is not produced by or for North Park University, and its questions should not be taken to imply any views of North Park University. Obviously, in a test of this type there are no "correct" answers. This test should be taken at the beginning of a semester and again at the end of the semester to assess change in image of Jesus and image of self.

Note: Your professor will never know who answered what on this test.

Part 1
What Do *You* Think of Jesus?

Please answer each question with a "yes" (Y) or "no" (N). Work quickly and do not think too long about the exact meaning of the questions. Please answer this Part 1 for what *you* think about Jesus.

1. Does his mood often go up and down?   Y   N

2. Is he a talkative person?   Y   N

3. Would being in debt worry him?   Y   N

4. Is he rather lively?   Y   N

5. Was he ever greedy by helping himself to more than his share of anything?   Y   N

* North England Institute for Christian Education

6. Would he take drugs that may have strange
   or dangerous effects?   Y   N

7. Has he ever blamed someone for doing something
   he knew was really his fault?   Y   N

8. Does he prefer to go his own way rather than act
   by the rules?   Y   N

9. Does he often feel "fed-up"?   Y   N

10. Has he ever taken anything (even a pin or button)
    that belonged to someone else?   Y   N

11. Would he call himself a nervous person?   Y   N

12. Does he think marriage is old-fashioned and should
    be done away with?   Y   N

13. Can he easily get some life into a rather dull party?   Y   N

14. Is he a worrier?   Y   N

15. Does he tend to keep in the background on social
    occasions?   Y   N

16. Does it worry him if he knows there are mistakes
    in his work?   Y   N

17. Has he ever cheated at a game?   Y   N

18. Does he suffer from "nerves"?   Y   N

19. Has he ever taken advantage of someone?   Y   N

20. Is he mostly quiet when he is with other people?   Y   N

21. Does he often feel lonely?   Y   N

22. Does he think it is better to follow society's rules
    than go his own way?   Y   N

23. Do other people think of him as being very lively?   Y   N

24. Does he always practice what he preaches?   Y   N

Part 2

Who Are You?

25. Which sex are you?
   ☐ Female   ☐ Male

26. What is your age?
   ☐ 18–19   ☐ 20–21   ☐ 22–23   ☐ 24–25   ☐ older than 25

27. Which school year are you in?
   ☐ Freshman   ☐ Sophomore   ☐ Junior   ☐ Senior

28. Are you taking this BTS course to fulfill General Education requirements?
   ☐ Yes   ☐ No

29. Which denomination to do you belong to?
   ☐ Covenant   ☐ Roman Catholic   ☐ Evangelical
   ☐ Pentecostal-charismatic   ☐ Mainline Protestant.

30. Do you go to church …
   ☐ weekly   ☐ at least once a month   ☐ sometimes
   ☐ once or twice per year   ☐ never?

Part 3

What Do *You* Think About *Yourself*?

[Do not look at your answers to questions 1–24.]

31. Does your mood often go up and down?   Y   N

32. Are you a talkative person?   Y   N

33. Would being in debt worry you?   Y   N

34. Are you rather lively?   Y   N

35. Were you ever greedy by helping himself to more
    than your share of anything?   Y   N

36. Would you take drugs which may have strange
    or dangerous effects?   Y   N

37. Have you ever blamed someone for doing something you knew was really your fault?   Y   N

38. Do you prefer to go your own way rather than act by the rules?   Y   N

39. Do you often feel "fed-up"?   Y   N

40. Have you ever taken anything (even a pin or button) that belonged to someone else?   Y   N

41. Would you call yourself a nervous person?   Y   N

42. Do you think marriage is old-fashioned and should be done away with?   Y   N

43. Can you easily get some life into a rather dull party?   Y   N

44. Are you a worrier?   Y   N

45. Do you tend to keep in the background on social occasions?   Y   N

46. Does it worry you if you know there are mistakes in your work?   Y   N

47. Have you ever cheated at a game?   Y   N

48. Do you suffer from "nerves"?   Y   N

49. Have you ever taken advantage of someone?   Y   N

50. Are you mostly quiet when you are with other people?   Y   N

51. Do you often feel lonely?   Y   N

52. Do you think it is better to follow society's rules than go your own way?   Y   N

53. Do other people think of you as being very lively?   Y   N

54. Do you always practice what you preach?   Y   N

1 Corinthians 14:34–35

One solution that ends every problem for the silencing of women in 1 Corinthians 14:34–35 is to argue that Paul did not even write these words. If you look carefully at your Bible (and I'm using the TNIV), you may observe a small footnote letter at the end of 1 Corinthians 14:35. At the bottom of this page in my Bible a footnote reads "*34, 35* In some manuscripts these verses come after verse 40." In my copy of *The Harper Collins Study Bible* on the NRSV, verses 34 and 35 are enclosed in parentheses and a note similar to the TNIV is found as a footnote. Most modern Bibles inform the reader that there is a problem about where these verses were originally located, and some experts conclude that they were not in Paul's original letter at all.

Why do they conclude this? Three reasons:

1. All attentive readers will feel the seeming contradiction between Paul's words here and what Paul said earlier in this very letter about women praying and prophesying in public. Something unusual is going on here.
2. Furthermore, verses 34 and 35 at face value overtly contradict the actual ministry conduct of women in the earliest churches. Women weren't completely silent in churches.
3. Some early manuscripts put these verses in another location, probably because they did not seem to fit between verses 33 and 36. Gordon Fee is one of evangelicalism's finest scholars. He is also a world-class expert on textual matters, and he is a leading scholar on 1 Corinthians itself. Fee, bringing all of his expertise to bear on these verses, came to the conclusion that *Paul did not*

write these verses, that someone added them to a margin of an early manuscript, and that from there they found their way into 1 Corinthians in two different locations.[1] If Fee and others like him are right, these verses, and not women, need to be silenced! But, many are not so sure Fee is right.

The singular problem Gordon Fee faces is that there is no manuscript evidence that these verses were ever omitted from any of the copies we have of 1 Corinthians. The statement about silence always shows up, either after verse 33 or after verse 40. So, the majority thinks these two verses should be included.[2] For that reason, I chose to ignore this problem and explain the text as if it where authentic to Paul.

Appendix 4

Petronius on the New Roman Woman

I want to quote a section from one of Rome's famous contemporaries of the apostle Paul, a man named Petronius, who describes what many today are calling the new Roman woman.[1] Who was Petronius? He was Emperor Nero's advisor in luxury and extravagance! Petronius describes the new Roman woman by speaking of the woman Fortunata at a dinner banquet where she and another woman, Scintilla, fall into admiration of themselves.

Fortunata greets Scintilla:

> At this [Fortunata] entered at last, her frock kilted up with a yellow girdle, so as to show a cherry-colored tunic underneath, and corded anklets and gold-embroidered slippers. Then wiping her hands on a handkerchief she wore at her neck, she placed herself on the same couch beside Habinnas' wife, Scintilla, kissing her while the other claps her hands, and exclaiming, "Have I really the pleasure of seeing you?"

Fortunata displays gold jewelry:

> Before long it came to Fortunata's taking off the bracelets from her great fat arms to show them to her admiring companion. Finally she even undid her anklets and her hairnet, which she assured Scintilla was of the very finest gold.

Trimalchio speaks of the women's extravagances:

> Trimalchio, observing this, ordered all the things to be brought to him. "You see this woman's fetters," he cried; "that's the way we poor devils are robbed! Six pound and a half, if it's an ounce; and yet I've got one myself of ten pound weight, all made out of Mercury's thousandths." Eventually to prove he was not telling a lie, he ordered a pair of scales to be brought, and had the articles carried round and the weight tested by each in turn.

Scintilla shows a jewelry box:

> And Scintilla was just as bad, for she drew from her bosom a little gold casket she called her Lucky Box. From it she produced a pair of ear-pendants and handed them one after the other to Fortunata to admire, saying, "Thanks to my husband's goodness, no wife has finer."

Tipsy women:

> Meanwhile the two women, though a trifle piqued, laughed good humoredly together and interchanged some tipsy kisses, the one praising the thrifty management of the lady of the house, the other enlarging on the minions her husband kept and his unthrifty ways. While they were thus engaged in close confabulation, Habinnas got up stealthily and catching hold of Fortunata's legs, upset her on the couch. "Ah! ah!" she screeched, as her tunic slipped up above her knees. Then falling on Scintilla's bosom, she hid in her handkerchief a face all afire with blushes.

Appendix 5

Juvenal on First-Century Women

To give an example of Roman women being educated, quite well in some cases, I want to quote from Juvenal,[1] another first-century Roman contemporary of Paul, who writes satirically about women. What is so interesting about this text is what it reveals about what women could do when it came to public teaching and discourse. Also, this text shows that Paul's strategy of educating women was in sharp contrast with some public opinions of women.

Asserting authority

> But most intolerable of all is the woman who as soon as she has sat down to dinner commends Virgil, pardons the dying Dido, and pits the poets against each other, putting Virgil in the one scale and Homer in the other. The grammarians make way before her; the rhetoricians give in; the whole crowd is silenced: no lawyer, no auctioneer will get a word in, no, nor any other woman; so torrential is her speech that you would think that all the pots and bells were being clashed together.... She lays down definitions, and discourses on morals, like a philosopher; thirsting to be deemed both wise and eloquent, she ought to tuck up her skirts knee-high, sacrifice a pig to Silvanus, take a penny bath.

Advice: limit the education of women

> Let not the wife of your bosom possess a special style of her own; let her not hurl at you in whirling speech the crooked enthymeme! Let her not know all history; let there be some things in her reading which she does not understand. I hate a woman who is for ever consulting and poring over the "Grammar" of Palaemon, who observes all the rules and laws of language, who like an antiquary quotes verses that I never heard of, and corrects her unlettered female friends for slips of speech that no man need trouble about: let husbands at least be permitted to make slips in grammar!

Notes

Chapter 1. The Book and I

1. Of course, I know many scholars have defended our current Christian practice; some of these are ingenious and profound and the like, but the implications we draw from some New Testament texts are not what the earliest Christians drew from them (as far as we know). The early Christians, especially the earliest Jewish Christians, continued to practice Sabbath alongside Sunday worship. For some New Testament references to Sabbath practice, see Acts 16:13; 18:4; 20:7; 1 Corinthians 16:2. Paul tolerated Gentile difference (Colossians 2:16) but Sabbath was not abandoned probably until the time of Constantine.

2. William D. Mounce, *Pastoral Epistles* (Word Biblical Commentary; Dallas: Word, 2000), 289.

Chapter 2. The Birds and I

1. I swiped this from this website: www-personal.umich.edu/~bbowman/birds/humor/birdrif6.html.

2. Tokunboh Adeyemo, ed., *Africa Bible Commentary* (Grand Rapids: Zondervan, 2006).

3. C. C. Kroeger, M. J. Evans, and E. K. Elliott, eds., *The IVP Women's Bible Commentary* (Downers Grove, IL: InterVarsity Press, 2002).

4. T. Oden, *The Rebirth of Orthodoxy* (San Francisco: HarperSanFrancisco, 2003); J. I. Packer and T. Oden, *One Faith: The Evangelical Consensus* (Downers Grove, IL: InterVarsity Press, 2004); C. Colson, *The Faith* (Grand Rapids: Zondervan, 2008).

5. There are two series of commentaries underway designed to do just this for Bible readers: *The Ancient Christian Commentary on Scripture* from InterVarsity Press and *The Church's Bible* from Eerdmans. Of course, there are oodles of options here, but one can use the *Ante-Nicene Fathers* and *Nicene and Post-Nicene Fathers* from Eerdmans, and then read Augustine and Aquinas and Luther and Calvin and Wesley and various others up to the modern day. One cannot read each of these for each sitting with the Bible, but it is our ongoing exposure to the past that creates in us a serious respect.

Chapter 3. Inkblots and Puzzles

1. Edith Humphrey, *Ecstasy and Intimacy* (Grand Rapids: Eerdmans, 2006), 41.

2. A pastor friend of mine, John Frye, wrote a novel explaining this very thing. It is called *Out of Print* (Grand Rapids: Credo House, 2007).

3. In my text in Appendix 2, there are no right answers; the score correlates similarities between how we view Jesus and how we view ourselves. For the studies, see L. J. Francis and J. Astley, "The Quest for the Psychological Jesus: Influences of Personality on Images of Jesus," *Journal of Psychology and Christianity* 16 (1997): 247–59; J. Astley and L. J. Francis, "A Level Gospel Study and Adolescents' Images of Jesus," in L. J. Francis, W. K. Kay, and W. S. Campbell, *Research in Religious Education* (Herefordshire, England: Gracewing, 1996), 239–47. Available online at: http://books.google.com/books?hl=en&id=n4Pmb9ik3GgC&dq=research+in +religious+education+leslie+j+francis&printsec=frontcover&source=web&ots=CvRMG4mvpX &sig=bhadoHLZcAHuZtdtFCt0ev27sCc#PPP2,M1

4. Mark Twain, *The Bible according to Mark Twain*, ed. H. G. Baetzhold and J. B. McCullough (New York: Simon & Schuster [Touchstone], 1996), 139.

5. Eugene Peterson, *Eat This Book: A Conversation in the Art of Spiritual Reading* (Grand Rapids: Baker, 2006), 66.

Chapter 4. It's a Story with Power!

1. Robert Webber, *The Divine Embrace* (Grand Rapids: Baker Academic, 2007), 128.

2. John Goldingay, *Old Testament Theology*; Volume 1: *Israel's Gospel* (Downers Grove, IL: InterVarsity Press, 2003), 31.

3. Abraham Joshua Heschel, *Moral Grandeur and Spiritual Audacity*, ed. S. Heschel (New York: Farrar, Straus, & Giroux, 1996), 12–13.

4. See Alister McGrath, *Christianity's Dangerous Idea* (New York: HarperOne, 2007).

5. For Tyndale, I have relied on David Daniell, *William Tyndale: A Biography* (New Haven: Yale Univ. Press, 1994). Quotations and allusions are from pp. 1, 141, 148, 182, 279, 319, 381, 383.

6. Goldingay, *Old Testament Theology*, 1:24.

Chapter 5. The Plot of the Wiki-Stories

1. It is impossible to know how many "authors" are involved in the composing of the thirty-nine Old Testament books. Since it likely that one author wrote more than one book (say 1–2 Samuel and 1–2 Kings and 1–2 Chronicles), I have simply said there are at least thirty authors.

2. Irenaeus, *On the Apostolic Preaching*, trans. J. Behr (Crestwood, NY: St. Vladimir's Seminary Press, 1997).

3. The Hebrew word translated "image" is *tselem* and the one translated "likeness" is *demut*. The word *tselem* was translated into Greek as *Eikon*, and because Jesus is the Perfect *Eikon* in the New Testament and because the expression "image of God" has endured constant battles over its precise meanings, I have been using *Eikon* instead of "image of God."

4. Mark Twain, *The Autobiography of Mark Twain*, ed. C. Neider (New York: HarperCollins, 1990), 277.

Chapter 7. God Speaks, We Listen

1. Dave Isay, *Listening Is an Act of Love* (New York: Penguin, 2007). I've not read this book.

2. Alan Jacobs, *A Theology of Reading: The Hermeneutics of Love* (Boulder, CO: Westview, 2001).

3. Ibid., 13.

4. Klyne Snodgrass, "Reading to Hear: A Hermeneutics of Hearing," *Horizons in Biblical Theology* 24 (2002): 1–32.

Chapter 8. The Boring Chapter
(on Missional Listening)

1. Scholars think he began this work late in the fourth century and finished in AD 427.

2. This is the title of Gordon Fee and Douglas Stuart's book, *How to Read the Bible for All It's Worth* (Grand Rapids: Zondervan, 2003).

3. *On Christian Doctrine*, trans. and intro. by D. W. Robertson Jr. (Upper Saddle River, NJ: Prentice Hall, 1997), 30–31. Later in this work Augustine defines "charity" as "the motion of the soul toward the enjoyment of God for His own sake, and the enjoyment of one's self and one's neighbor for the sake of God" (88).

4. P. H. Towner, *The Letters to Timothy and Titus* (New International Commentary on the New Testament; Grand Rapids: Eerdmans, 2006), 581.

5. This translation seeks to show the chiasm of 2 Timothy 3:16. There are four elements, and the first and the fourth are together and the second and third are together. Thus,

A Inform (*didaskalia*)

B Rebuke (*elegmon*)

B' Restore (*epanorthosis*)

A' Instruct (*paideia in dikaiosune*)

6. The TNIV has a note after "so that all God's people" that reads, "Or *that the servant of God*." The Greek text, in a more literal rendering, reads "so that the *man of God* may be ..." Rendering this "all God's people," which I think is correct, recognizes that Paul's comments were intended to apply to more than just Timothy but also to Timothy's churches—both males and females, both laity and clergy.

Chapter 9. The Year of Living Jesus-ly

1. A. J. Jacobs, *The Year of Living Biblically: One Man's Humble Quest to Follow the Bible as Literally as Possible* (New York: Simon and Schuster, 2007).

2. Ibid., 4.

3. Ibid., 6–7.

4. Ibid., 8.

5. Ibid., 328.

6. See my piece online: www.christianvisionproject.com/2008/03/the_8_marks_of_a _robust_gospel.html

The paper copy can be found at *Christianity Today* (March 2008), 36–39.

Chapter 10. Finding the Pattern of Discernment

1. For an excellent study, see David Instone-Brewer, *Divorce and Remarriage in the Bible: The Social and Literary Context* (Grand Rapids: Eerdmans, 2002); see also his online piece at www. christianitytoday.com/ct/2007/october/20.26.html.

2. There is serious dispute if this "exception" was granted by Jesus explicitly or if Matthew, knowing what Jesus meant, clarified it later. I consider the exception clause to be accurate for what Jesus meant.

3. Many manuscripts do not include this text, but most experts think it records an actual event in Jesus' life.

4. Gordon Fee, *The First Epistle to the Corinthians* (Grand Rapids: Eerdmans, 1987), 423.

Part 4. Women in Church Ministries Today

1. Scot McKnight, *Galatians* (NIV Application Commentary; Grand Rapids: Zondervan, 1995), 201–11; Scot McKnight, *1 Peter* (NIV Application Commentary; Grand Rapids: Zondervan, 1996), 180–98.

Chapter 11. The Bible and Women

1. This text is normally cited as Tosefta Berakot 7.18, but my edition of the Tosefta has it at Berakot 6.18. I use J. Neusner, *The Tosefta* (2 vols.; Peabody, MA: Hendrickson, 2002).

2. This saying, with variants, can be found in Diogenes Laertius, *Vitae Philosophorum* 1.33; Plutarch, *Marius* 46.1; Lactantius, *Divine Institutes* 3.19.17.

3. See *Dictionary of the Old Testament: Pentateuch*, ed. T. Desmond Alexander and D. W. Baker (Downers Grove, IL: InterVarsity Press, 2003), 897–904; *Dictionary of the Old Testament: Historical Books*, ed. B. T. Arnold and H. G. M. Williamson (Downers Grove, IL: InterVarsity Press, 2005), 989–99; *Dictionary of the New Testament Background*, ed. C. A. Evans and S. E. Porter (Downers Grove, IL: InterVarsity Press, 2000), 1276–80.

4. See *Dictionary of Jesus and the Gospels*, ed. J. B. Green, S. McKnight, and I. H. Marshall (Downers Grove, IL: InterVarsity Press, 1992), 880–87; I quote from p. 880.

5. Josephus, *Against Apion* 2.201.

6. A brief sketch of this can be found in Sarah Sumner, *Men and Women in the Church* (Downers Grove, IL: InterVarsity Press, 2003), 58–69.

7. A small sampling, even if not representing the more negative side, can be found in Mark J. Edwards, *Ancient Christian Commentary on Scripture*, vol. 8: *Galatians, Ephesians, Philippians* (Downers Grove, IL: InterVarsity Press, 1999), 183–90.

8. See Ruth A. Tucker and Walter Liefeld, *Daughters of the Church* (Grand Rapids: Zondervan, 1987).

9. The best sketch of this I have seen is William Webb, *Slaves, Women and Homosexuals: Exploring the Hermeneutics of Cultural Analysis* (Downers Grove, IL: InterVarsity Press, 2001), 22 – 29, upon which I have relied in this section.

10. I don't like the term "egalitarianism" because it smacks too much of an Enlightenment sense of rights and justice and less of the biblical sense of mutuality designed in creation and reestablished in new creation. I believe there is something real in femininity and masculinity that distinguishes women from men, though I cannot define what that might be. I believe "mutuality" encourages a profound unity, equality, and distinctiveness better than the term "egalitarian." The term "egalitarian" conveys a battle while the term "mutuality" conveys partnership, companionship, and unity.

11. See Edwards, *Galatians, Ephesians, Philippians*, 190 (quoting Chrysostom).

Chapter 12. What Did Women Do in the Old Testament?

1. I am deeply aware of the amount and depth of scholarship on the many passages I will mention in what follows, but in this context it is not remotely possible to enter into the many debates. I recommend the following books for your own personal study: R. W. Pierce and R. M. Groothuis, eds., *Discovering Biblical Equality: Complementarity without Hierarchy* (Downers Grove, IL: InterVarsity Press, 2005); A. Mickelsen, ed., *Women, Authority and the Bible* (Downers Grove, IL: InterVarsity Press, 1986); B. Clouse and R. G. Clouse, eds., *Women in Ministry: Four Views* (Downers Grove, IL: InterVarsity Press, 1989); James R. Beck, ed., *Two Views on Women in Ministry*, rev. ed. (Grand Rapids: Zondervan, 2005); S. Sumner, *Men and Women in the Church* (Downers Grove, IL: InterVarsity Press, 2003); J. Stackhouse, *Finally Feminist: A Pragmatic Christian Understanding of Gender* (Grand Rapids: Baker, 2005); R. T. France, *Women in the Church's Ministry: A Test Case for Biblical Interpretation* (Grand Rapids: Eerdmans, 1995); B. Witherington III, *Women in the Ministry of Jesus* (Cambridge: Cambridge Univ. Press, 1987) and *Women in the Earliest Churches* (Cambridge: Cambridge Univ. Press, 1991).

2. From Peter J. Leithart, *1 and 2 Kings* (Grand Rapids: Brazos, 2006), 267.

Chapter 13. What Did Women Do in the New Testament?

1. See my *The Real Mary* (Brewster, MA: Paraclete, 2006).

2. For the sake of completeness, I do not see the same influence in the book of Jude, which tradition claims was written by another son of Mary.

3. An unbiased sifting of the evidence can be found in D. J. Moo, *The Epistle to the Romans* (Grand Rapids: Eerdmans, 1996), 921 – 23; an exhaustive study by a specialist in textual criticism is E. J. Epp, *Junia: The First Woman Apostle* (Minneapolis: Fortress, 2005).

4. Moo, *Romans*, 923 – 24.

5. Other "co-workers" can be found at Romans 16:9, 21; 1 Corinthians 3:9; 2 Corinthians 8:23; Philippians 2:25; 4:2 – 3; 1 Thessalonians 3:2; Philemon 1, 24.

6. See 1 Corinthians 3:5 – 9: "What, after all, is Apollos? And what is Paul? Only servants,

through whom you came to believe—as the Lord has assigned to each his task. I planted the seed, Apollos watered it, but God has been making it grow. So neither the one who plants nor the one who waters is anything, but only God, who makes things grow. The one who plants and the one who waters have one purpose, and they will each be rewarded according to their own labor. For we are God's co-workers; you are God's field, God's building."

7. Moo, *Romans*, 914.

8. An imaginative approach to Romans can be found in Reta Halteman Finger, *Roman House Churches for Today* (Grand Rapids: Eerdmans, 2007).

9. R. Jewett, *Romans* (Minneapolis: Fortress, 2007), 947–48.

10. The technical discussion for what I state here can be found in G. H. R. Horsley, *New Documents Illustrating Early Christianity* (Macquarie, Australia: Macquarie Univ. Press, 1987), 4:239–44.

Chapter 14. Silencing the Blue Parakeet (1)

1. For a more technical defense of this, see Susan Foh, "What Is the Woman's Desire?" *Westminster Theological Journal* 37 (1974–75): 376–83; but see also the excellent study of Richard S. Hess, "Equality with and without Innocence: Genesis 1–3," in *Discovering Biblical Equality: Complementarity without Hierarchy*, ed. R. W. Pierce and R. M. Groothuis (Downers Grove, IL: InterVarsity Press, 2005), 79–95.

2. See Appendix 3 for a special problem with these verses.

3. C. S. Keener, "Learning in the Assemblies: 1 Corinthians 14:34–35," in *Discovering Biblical Equality*, 161–71.

4. There are basically two views of this passage and, in fact, of women in ministry; one sides with the Restorationist and Roman Catholic views of how we read the Bible and the other sides with the reformed and always reforming view. The former is often called "complementarian" and the latter "egalitarian," though simple labels mask both the seriousness of the views as well as nuances within and between such views. The term "complementarian" fudges the reality; this view is really a "hierarchical" view, for the focus is on male leadership and female subordination. I am both with the reformed and always reforming view, and while I can be labeled an "egalitarian," I prefer to use other terms for my view of women in ministry. Two technical studies of this passage, the first from the complementarian side and the second from the egalitarian side, are W. D. Mounce, *Pastoral Epistles* (Word Biblical Commentary; Nashville: Nelson, 2000), 94–149, including eight dense pages of bibliography; Towner, *The Letters to Timothy and Titus*, 190–239.

Chapter 15. Silencing the Blue Parakeet (2)

1. On this, see especially B. W. Winter, *Roman Wives, Roman Widows: The Appearance of New Women and the Pauline Communities* (Grand Rapids: Eerdmans, 2003). Phil Towner, in his excellent commentary on the Pastoral Epistles, has sifted through recent studies on the context at Ephesus and brings them all to bear upon this passage in his extensive, excellent analysis; see *The Letters to Timothy and Titus*, 190–239.

2. See the discussion in Winter, *Roman Wives, Roman Widows*, 39–58.

3. Towner, *The Letters to Timothy and Titus*, 239.

Appendix 3. 1 Corinthians 14:34–35

1. See Gordon Fee, *The First Epistle to the Corinthians* (Grand Rapids: Eerdmans, 1987), 699–708; Fee expanded his arguments in his book *God's Empowering Presence* (Peabody, MA: Hendrickson, 1994), 272–81. These issues are complex and few have taken Fee on at the level of his expertise.

2. I believe Fee got this right, but many of my readers will not agree with Fee, so I have pursued this argument in a different direction.

Appendix 4. Petronius on the New Roman Woman

1. I use the online edition of Petronius, *Satyricon*, found at www.igibud.com/petron/satyr/satyr.txt. Another translation of this Latin text can be found at Petronius, *Satyricon* (Cambridge, MA: Harvard Univ. Press, 1987), section 67.

Appendix 5. Juvenal on First-Century Women

1. I use the online of edition of Juvenal, *Satire 6*, found at http://en.wikisource.org/wiki/Satire_6. Another translation can be found at Juvenal, *Satires* (Cambridge, MA: Harvard Univ. Press, 1961), 434–56.

Willow Creek Association

Vision, Training, Resources for Prevailing Churches

This resource was created to serve you and to help you build a local church that prevails. It is just one of many ministry tools that are part of the Willow Creek Resources® line, published by the Willow Creek Association together with Zondervan.

The Willow Creek Association (WCA) was created in 1992 to serve a rapidly growing number of churches from across the denominational spectrum that are committed to helping unchurched people become fully devoted followers of Christ. Membership in the WCA now numbers over 12,000 Member Churches worldwide from more than ninety denominations.

The Willow Creek Association links like-minded Christian leaders with each other and with strategic vision, training, and resources in order to help them build prevailing churches designed to reach their redemptive potential. Here are some of the ways the WCA does that.

- **The Leadership Summit**—a once a year, two-and-a-half-day conference to envision and equip Christians with leadership gifts and responsibilities. Presented live at Willow Creek as well as via satellite broadcast to over 130 locations across North America, this event is designed to increase the leadership effectiveness of pastors, ministry staff, volunteer church leaders, and Christians in the marketplace.

- **Ministry-Specific Conferences** — throughout each year the WCA hosts a variety of conferences and training events — both at Willow Creek's main campus and offsite, across the U.S., and around the world — targeting church leaders and volunteers in ministry-specific areas such as: small groups, preaching and teaching, the arts, children, students, volunteers, stewardship, etc.

- **Willow Creek Resources®** — provides churches with trusted and field-tested ministry resources in such areas as leadership, evangelism, spiritual formation, spiritual gifts, small groups, stewardship, student ministry, children's ministry, the use of the arts — drama, media, contemporary music — and more.

- **WCA Member Benefits** — includes substantial discounts to WCA training events, a 20 percent discount on all Willow Creek Resources®, *Defining Moments* monthly audio journal for leaders, quarterly *Willow* magazine, access to a Members-Only section on WillowNet, monthly communications, and more. Member Churches also receive special discounts and premier services through WCA's growing number of ministry partners — Select Service Providers — and save an average of $500 annually depending on the level of engagement.

For specific information about WCA conferences, resources, membership, and other ministry services contact:

Willow Creek Association
P.O. Box 3188
Barrington, IL 60011-3188
Phone: 847-570-9812
Fax: 847-765-5046
www.willowcreek.com

Share Your Thoughts

With the Author: Your comments will be forwarded to
the author when you send them to *zauthor@zondervan.com*.

With Zondervan: Submit your review of this book
by writing to *zreview@zondervan.com*.

Free Online Resources at

www.zondervan.com/hello

Zondervan AuthorTracker: Be notified whenever your
favorite authors publish new books, go on tour, or post
an update about what's happening in their lives.

Daily Bible Verses and Devotions: Enrich your life
with daily Bible verses or devotions that help you start
every morning focused on God.

Free Email Publications: Sign up for newsletters on
fiction, Christian living, church ministry, parenting, and
more.

Zondervan Bible Search: Find and compare
Bible passages in a variety of translations at
www.zondervanbiblesearch.com.

Other Benefits: Register yourself to receive online
benefits like coupons and special offers, or to participate
in research.